AUDITING LOCAL UNION FINANCIAL RECORDS

A GUIDE FOR LOCAL UNION TRUSTEES

John Lund

Union Communication Services, Inc.
Annapolis, MD

333

Library of Congress Control Number: 2005908721

ISBN (10-digit): 0-9659486-3-3
ISBN (13-digit): 9780965948630

Also published by Union Communication Services, Inc.

The Union Steward's Complete Guide: A Survival Manual
Edited by David Prosten

The Union Member's Complete Guide: Everything You Want – and Need – to Know About Working Union
By Michael Mauer

Copies may be ordered from

Union Communication Services, Inc.
165 Conduit Street
Annapolis, MD 21401
1-800-321-2545
ucs@unionist.com
www.unionist.com

0987654321

Contents

List of Figures

Acknowledgments

"What is the local union trustee supposed to do?" Having heard this question perhaps one time too many, I decided to find the answer. I began by collecting union training manuals, union constitutions and bylaws, and union financial reporting forms; investigating Labor Department audit procedures; and, most important, talking with local union trustees and financial officers. Without the comments, criticisms, and suggestions of trustees and financial officers too numerous to mention here, this book would not have been possible. I'd also like to recognize the many helpful suggestions I've received from the Office of Labor-Management Standards, U.S. Department of Labor.

Well-informed and conscientious trustees and local auditors are the best defense against financial misunderstandings and potential misdeeds within their local unions. A more detailed LM form or additional enforcement by the Labor Department is no substitute here.

The question that I started asking in the early 1990s is still timely. Since this book was first published by ILR Press at Cornell University in 1992, thousands of union officers, trustees and auditors have read it and taken my classes, but many new financial officers and trustees have been elected and need the proper tools to do their job. My thanks go to Union Communication Services for recognizing this fact by republishing this book.

Finally, I dedicate this volume to my parents, Kjell and Effie Lund.

1

Introduction

☐ A review of payroll deduction records shows the employer has *underpaid* union dues for almost six months. The difference between the correct amount and the amount actually paid is $3,450.00. But before you can attempt to collect the difference, you realize the underpayment occurred *three years* ago!

☐ Before moving out of your old office and into a new one, you discover chairs, tables, filing cabinets, and two calculators are missing. A search of union records and property indicates when the items were purchased, but there is no record of their being sold or donated.

☐ Correspondence has been received from the U.S. Department of Labor, Office of Labor-Management Standards, and the Internal Revenue Service claiming that the local union did not file LM-2 and IRS 990 forms last year. The financial officer responsible for filing these forms has been on military leave since the end of last year.

☐ The president of the union needs a check immediately to pay for some office supplies. Picking up the checkbook, she notices from the register that three consecutive checks have been marked "void." After some looking, the voided checks turn up with the canceled checks with the monthly bank statements. The three canceled checks have been made out to cash and total $458.23.

☐ A steward has filed a claim for lost wages, but a member of the local union complains to you that this individual was also "on the clock" at work during the same period for which the lost wages are being claimed. Your review of payroll records, time cards, and lost wage vouchers reveals this is true and that this practice has been going on for some time.

The story is told of a local union financial officer giving some friendly advice to her newly elected successor. Handing the incoming financial officer *three* sealed envelopes, the veteran officer counseled, "When you find yourself in trouble with the local union's finances, open one of these letters. Each should see you through a crisis."

About six months into his new term of office, the financial officer was having problems with the books and masses of recordkeeping. In desperation, he opened the first letter. It said, "Blame everything on your predecessor." The new financial officer did so, and it worked like a charm, ending the crisis.

All was well for six months, when a new financial crisis erupted. The financial officer opened another letter. This one said, "Tell the membership that you understand there is a problem and that you are working hard to find a fair solution to it." The financial officer announced this at the next local union meeting and managed to put this crisis to rest.

All went well for six more months. Knowing that the advice in the letters had saved him twice before, the financial officer opened the third and final letter. Its advice was simple: "Write three letters."

As the preceding story and scenarios indicate, the job of the local union financial officer is not always an easy one. Besides keeping the books, there are union and government reports to file, accounts to manage, and many, many other details to administer. But the financial officer of the local union is not alone.

It is the job of the local union trustee or auditor to check local union records to ensure that all union funds, accounts, and assets have been handled properly and that accurate records have been maintained. In doing this job, the local union trustee or auditor performs a vitally important service to the local union and to the local union's financial officer.

A local union auditor or trustee may not have been able to prevent the above incidents from happening. But a trained and alert trustee or auditor should be able to recognize such problems and call them to the attention of the local union's financial officer or executive board so that *prompt* corrective action can be taken.

Goal of This Bulletin

The hope is that this bulletin will provide local union trustees and auditors with the know-how and confidence to spot problems so they can be promptly reported and corrected. This bulletin provides local union trustees and auditors with a basic road map of procedures and a toolbox of skills and worksheets to accomplish their jobs.

The precise duties and responsibilities of local union auditors or trustees vary from union to union. In some cases, the trustees or auditors are also members of the local union executive board; in some cases, they are not. The exact relationship between the trustees or auditors and the union's executive board varies, depending on union constitutions and bylaws.

The relationship between the trustee or auditor and the financial officer of the local union also varies from union to union and depends in part on the constitution and bylaws of the organization. It should *not*, however, be an *adversarial* relationship. It should be a *mutually supportive* relationship, in which the financial officer generates an audit trail and provides the trustees or auditors with *all* the necessary information to perform a speedy and complete audit.

In turn, the auditors or trustees should work cooperatively with the financial officers to help them do their jobs effectively. Trustees should not attempt to "get the goods" on the financial officer; nor should they see the financial officer as "trying to pull a fast one." What might appear to be a glaring inconsistency in the records may have a perfectly reasonable explanation. Trustees should avoid "knee-jerk" reactions to what look like problems. If something doesn't look right, the first thing a trustee or auditor should do is ask the financial officer about it. Financial officers should not see the auditors or trustees as a threat, but as another pair of eyes to review records and transactions to make sure nothing has been missed.

This bulletin is intended to assist local union trustees or auditors in the process of reviewing or auditing their local union's financial records. Although audit requirements and financial recordkeeping standards vary considerably from union to union, depending on their constitutions, bylaws, resolutions, and tradition, all audits should have some basic principles and procedures in common. This bulletin describes these general principles and then applies them to specific situations you are likely to encounter in an audit or review of local union financial records. **Where your own union's constitutional requirements differ from the instructions in this bulletin, you should follow the instructions and requirements of your union.** This book is *not* intended to replace or contradict any instructions local union trustees or auditors receive from their national or international union.

Before You Begin Your Audit

Before beginning your audit, you should *always* consult your constitution and bylaws to determine what rights and responsibilities you have as a local union trustee. You may also wish to consult your local union recording secretary, president, or *past* local union trustees or auditors. Another good source of information is your business agent, district or regional council office, or international representative. Some national or international unions have their own auditors who are also valuable resources.

The following questions are among those you should ask before you begin to review your local union records:

- ☐ To whom do I report the results of the audit? Is there a particular form or set of forms I should use?
- ☐ Whom do I contact if I have questions or need additional records?
- ☐ Whom should I contact if I uncover problems or discrepancies in the financial records?
- ☐ When will I conduct the audit, and when is the report due?
- ☐ Will I be compensated for any expenses, including lost wages, that I incur during the audit? If so, what are these expenses?

The answers to these questions will vary depending on which union you're in. In some cases your constitution and bylaws will be crystal clear, sometimes not. You should get these questions answered before you begin.

This bulletin does *not* cover the duties of joint labor-management trustees of joint labor-management Taft-Hartley trusts (pension, health, and welfare trusts). Trustees of such funds are governed by a different law, the Employee Retirement Income Security Act of 1974, and its regulations and case law.

The instructions and recommendations in this bulletin are generally applicable to both private and public sector labor organizations, subject, of course, to any specific constitutional and bylaw requirements for financial recordkeeping and reporting they may have.

Organization of This Bulletin

This bulletin is divided into five chapters.

Chapter 2 reviews the rights and responsibilities of local union trustees under both the Labor-Management Reporting and Disclosure Act (the Landrum-Griffin Act or LMRDA) of 1959 and outlines what those duties and responsibilities typically are under union constitutions and bylaws.

Chapter 3 reviews income sources, including union dues, initiation fees, fines, rents, sales of supplies, and assets. This chapter also discusses the duty of a union trustee or auditor to make certain that the local union receives every cent of income to which it is entitled and that all income is properly accounted for.

Chapter 4 covers assets, including *fixed* assets (property, vehicles, furniture, and office equipment) as well as *liquid* assets (savings and checking accounts, stocks and bonds, money market or mutual funds, and certificates of deposit). Guidelines for properly accounting for each type of asset are reviewed.

Chapter 5 focuses on disbursements. Before local union funds can be disbursed (spent), they must be *authorized*. Normally, this requires action by either the local union executive board or the membership. Additionally, proper *documentation* of these expenditures must be maintained to prove the funds were spent in accordance with the authorization. This chapter discusses what authorization and documentation trustees should normally expect to find and what other records should be reviewed.

Chapter 6, the final chapter, tackles three questions: How should you summarize the results of your audit or review? How should you present your report? And how should you handle discrepancies or problems you encounter in your audit or review?

How to Use This Bulletin

How you use this bulletin will depend on the level of your experience or training in audit procedures.

- ☐ New trustees or auditors may wish to read the entire bulletin, review the skills and forms, and use the exercises provided to practice those skills.
- ☐ More experienced trustees or auditors may wish to review certain chapters or skills and use the exercises as a refresher.
- ☐ Trustees or auditors, new or old, may wish to use some or all of the forms to assist them.
- ☐ Trustees or local union financial officers may wish to recommend or adopt changes in their recordkeeping or audit procedures after reading this bulletin.
- ☐ For those who receive training or instructions from their national or international unions, portions of this bulletin may serve as a useful *supplement.*
- ☐ Financial officers may find useful methods for establishing audit trails that could help trustees and auditors accomplish their jobs more efficiently.

Because audit and recordkeeping requirements of your local union are likely to vary somewhat and because of time limitations, it is not necessary that you follow each and every recommended step. Instead, you may want to pick out ideas or worksheets that improve your own methods and provide guidance in areas you currently do not examine.

It is hoped that this bulletin will provide trustees and auditors at the local union level with some basic tools and skills to help them perform more efficiently and effectively. When they perform well, trustees and auditors provide a very vital service, which is to assure the union and its members that their funds are properly collected, spent, and accounted for.

A Word about Computerized Financial Recordkeeping

More and more unions are using microcomputer software such as Peachtree® or Quicken® to computerize their financial recordkeeping. The use of such software should not make your job any more difficult. The financial officer should be able to prepare a *transaction history* of all cash and disbursement entries from the beginning to the ending dates of the audit period. You can then compare these entries against the bank and check balances and other audit trails discussed in this bulletin.

Exercises for Chapter 1

Write the answers to the following questions *after* you have discussed them with former trustees or auditors, executive board members, or chief financial or executive officers of your local union.

1. To whom do I report the results of the audit? Is there a particular form or set of forms I should use?

2. Whom do I contact if I have questions or need additional records?

3. Whom should I contact if I uncover problems or discrepancies in the financial records?

4. When will I conduct the audit, and when is the report due?

5. Will I be compensated for any expenses, including lost wages, that I incur during the audit? If so, what are these expenses?

2

Rights and Responsibilities of Local Union Trustees

The rights and responsibilities of local union trustees and auditors are outlined in two places: the Labor-Management Reporting and Disclosure Act, sometimes known as the Landrum-Griffin Act, after its 1959 congressional co-sponsors; and the union's constitution and bylaws.

You won't find the term *local union trustee* mentioned once in the Landrum-Griffin Act. But, although the law does not mention trustees by name, it does establish general responsibilities for trustees, auditors, and all union officers. The *specific* rights and responsibilities of local union trustees or auditors are probably spelled out in your union constitution and bylaws.

The Labor-Management Reporting and Disclosure Act

The Labor-Management Reporting and Disclosure Act is a complex law that deals with several subjects including the rights of local union members, financial reporting, elections, local union receivership (when local unions are put under temporary international or national direction because of extraordinary circumstances), and the fiduciary responsibilities of local union officers. Each of these subjects is covered under a separate *title* of the act.

The sections that directly concern the local union trustee are Titles II and V. Title II deals with financial reporting; Title V deals with fiduciary responsibilities of union officers. Each of these titles and their requirements is discussed below.

Financial Reporting Requirements

Every private or federal government sector labor union, as well as public employee local unions with one or more private sector union members, must file a financial report with the U.S. Department of Labor within ninety (90) days of the end of the union's fiscal year.

Unions with less than $100,000 in annual receipts will file form LM-3; those with annual receipts of $100,000 or more must file form LM-2.

LM-3 is considerably less detailed and shorter than LM-2. Regardless of the form filed, it must be signed by the president and treasurer of the local union and include the following information:

- ☐ assets and liabilities at the *beginning* and *end* of the fiscal year;
- ☐ all receipts for income and their sources (dues, interest, sales, etc.);
- ☐ salary, allowances, and expenses of officers and employees of the union;
- ☐ direct and indirect loans that total more than $250 per fiscal year to any officer, employee, or member of the local union;
- ☐ direct or indirect loans made to any business enterprise during the fiscal year; and
- ☐ other disbursements by type made by the local union during the fiscal year.

The records necessary to prepare each year's LM-2 or LM-3 must be maintained for a *minimum* of *five* (5) years after the form is filed, according to Section 206 of the LMRDA. Local trustees or auditors should verify that records going back at least five years are maintained.

Unions should make information shown on the LM forms available to their members upon request. Failure to provide a member access to such information without *just cause* may result in a lawsuit being brought by the member. The court can then open up the local union's books and records and award the member reasonable attorney fees (LMRDA Section 201[c]).

LM-2 and LM-3 forms become public record when they are filed with the U.S. Department of Labor. Any person can file a Freedom of Information Act request and pay reasonable copying fees to obtain copies of these forms. Employers and labor-management consultants frequently use information from the forms during organizing campaigns.

Finally, the law contains criminal penalties for knowingly including false statements or false entries on LM-2 or LM-3 forms.

Local union trustees typically are not involved in filing the LM-2 or LM-3 form, but it is strongly recommended that you verify that they have been filed with the Department of Labor in a timely fashion. You should also verify that IRS 990 has been filed with the Internal Revenue Service (IRS). While there are no civil penalties for failing to file the LM-2 or LM-3 form in a timely manner, the IRS does impose penalties for failure to file the IRS 990 form on time. Form 990 must be filed no later than the fifteenth day of the fifth month following the fiscal year. This form is required of all unions with $25,000 or more in annual income.

Fiduciary Responsibilities

Section 501 of Title V of the act sets out the fiduciary responsibilities of union officers. This fiduciary responsibility extends to "officers, agents, shop stewards, and other representatives of a labor organization." These individuals, according to the law, "occupy positions of trust in relation to such organization and its members as a group." The *fiduciary duty* of union officers to the local union and its members is stated as follows:

> (1) *to hold its money and property solely for the benefit of the organization and its members,*
>
> (2) *to manage, invest, and expend the same in accordance with its constitution and bylaws and any resolutions of the governing bodies adopted thereunder,*
>
> (3) *to refrain from dealing with such organization as an adverse party* or in behalf of an adverse party in any matter connected with his duties and from holding or acquiring any pecuniary or personal interest which conflicts with the interests of such organization, and to account to the organization for any profit received by him in whatever capacity in connection with transactions conducted by him or under his direction on behalf of the organization (LMRDA Section 501[a], emphasis added).

Most, if not all, of these duties are spelled out in international or national union constitutions and bylaws. Violations of these duties are enforceable through internal union action. That they are included in the Landrum-Griffin Act makes them subject to enforcement *outside* the union as well.

Section 501(b) establishes the procedure for handling alleged violations of this *fiduciary responsibility*. Any member of the local union may demand that its local union or executive board investigate alleged breaches of this fiduciary responsibility by any officer of the local union. If these charges are investigated and found to be valid, the local union or its executive board is required by law to recover any misappropriated funds, demand a full accounting of them, or obtain other appropriate remedy within a *reasonable period of time.* If this is not done, the member who alleged the breach of fiduciary duties may bring suit against the local union in federal court. If the court decides the case in favor of the member, the court may award reasonable attorney fees in addition to the remedy sought by the member.

Finally, Section 501(c) establishes that any union officer who

> embezzles, steals, or unlawfully and willfully abstracts or converts to his own use, or the use of another, any of the moneys, funds, securities, property, or other assets of a labor organization of which he is an officer, or by which he is employed, directly or indirectly, shall be fined not more than $10,000 or imprisoned for not more than five years, or both.

There are several key points local union trustees should keep in mind from the preceding:

- ☐ All union officers, including trustees, occupy positions of trust.
- ☐ All union officers, including trustees, must hold the money and property of the local union *solely for the benefit of the local union and its members.*
- ☐ All union officers and trustees must ensure that funds of the local union are *managed, invested, and spent in accordance with the constitution, bylaws, and resolutions* of the local and parent union.
- ☐ All local union officers, including trustees, must avoid *conflicts of interest* in dealing with the local union.
- ☐ When this fiduciary trust is violated, the local union needs to take prompt action to demand an accounting and/or repayment within a reasonable time. If the union fails to take such action, any member may sue the officer(s) in court to recover payment or an accounting.
- ☐ Any officer who embezzles, steals, or converts union funds or property to his or her own use may be subject to criminal prosecution.

Local union trustees should be familiar with the bonding requirements of Section 502, which requires local union officers or employees who handle funds or property to be bonded in the amount of not less than 10 percent of the funds they or their predecessors handled in the previous fiscal year. You should make certain that all officers and employees who need to be are bonded adequately.

The bonding company must be selected from a list of acceptable firms maintained by the U.S. Department of Labor. You should contact your national or international union regarding bonding; it may have an arrangement with a specific company to provide bonding or have a list of acceptable bonding firms. Normally the office of the national or international secretary-treasurer is responsible for this function.

What Your Constitution and Bylaws Say about Trustees

Before you go any further, check your constitution and bylaws carefully for any mention of the rights and responsibilities of local union trustees. Below is an example of what one union constitution says:

> ☐ It shall be the duty of the Trustees to have *supervision over all funds and property of the Local Union* under such instructions as they shall from time to time receive from the Local Union;
>
> ☐ to see that the *funds of the Local Union are deposited* by the proper officers in such banks and accounts therein as the Local Union shall designate;
>
> ☐ to *examine the bank books and records* of the Treasurer and any other officer holding funds of the Local Union and see that the same are correct;
>
> ☐ to be *custodians of the bonds* covering the Financial-Secretary and Treasurer and such other officers as the Local Union may require to be bonded;
>
> ☐ to furnish the General President full and complete information on any subject within his control or knowledge when requested;
>
> ☐ In those instances in which the Local Union is audited not less than annually by an independent public accountant, the Trustees shall certify on the basis of the audit of such independent public accountant (Constitution and bylaws, International Union of Operating Engineers, AFL-CIO, Article XXIV, Subdivision 2, Section [h], emphasis added).

In the constitution from which the excerpt above is taken, trustees are given very significant general authority over finances, but there is no timetable or format imposed on them as to when and how the audit must be performed. In the following excerpt, many of the same general duties are mentioned, but the timing of the audit and how the audit report must be provided to the membership are defined.

> The Trustees shall have the supervision of all the funds and property of the Local, subject to such instructions as they can receive from time to time from the Local. It shall be the duty of the Trustees to see that the Financial Secretary-Treasurer deposits in such bank as the Local may decide all money over and above such sum as the Local shall decide may remain in his hands for contingent expenses and legal bills, instructing the officers of the bank to pay no money on account of the Local except as the Local may decide. The Trustees shall examine the bank book of the Financial Secretary-Treasurer annually, and see that it is correct and shall report annually to the Local and shall prepare and exercise in such sums as the Local may direct of the Financial Secretary-Treasurer, and shall perform such other duties as the Local may direct. All bills must be approved by the Trustees unless otherwise ordered by the organization.
>
> The Trustees shall at least yearly publish a complete audit of the funds and property of the Local and distribute such audit by mail to all members in good standing at their last known address (Constitution and bylaws, International Union of Elevator Constructors, Local 15, Milwaukee).

As the next example illustrates, some international unions provide local union trustees with standard forms for the audit. In this case, time limits for the audit are also established.

> The Trustees shall have general supervision over all funds and property of the Local Union. They shall audit the records of the Financial Officers of the Local Union once each month using duplicate forms provided by the International Union, a copy of which shall be forwarded to the International Secretary-Treasurer immediately thereafter. It shall also be their duty to see that the Financial Officers of the Local Union are bonded in conformity with the laws of the International Union. The Trustees shall see that all funds shall be deposited in a bank in the name of the Local Union, subject to an order or check signed by the President and the Financial Secretary-Treasurer of

> the Local Union. In the event the books are not received for audit within fifteen (15) days after the end of each month, the Chairperson of the Trustees shall immediately notify the International Secretary-Treasurer, and report the fact to the next meeting of the Local Union (Constitution, International Union of the Allied Industrial Workers, Article 29.05).

Finally, the *Bylaws for Local Unions* of the United Steelworkers of America require trustees

> to audit the books and financial records of the Local Union *every three months* and give a report of such audit at the next regular Local Union meeting. They shall perform such other duties as the Local Union may require. The Trustees should give special attention when checking disbursements recorded by the Financial Secretary and Treasurer that proper authorization for such payments have been entered by the Recording Secretary in the Minutes of the Local Union (page 25, emphasis added.)

You should read your constitution and bylaws carefully. It may be useful to attach a copy to the inside cover of this bulletin. You may not find all the information you need in your constitution and bylaws. You may need to ask specific questions of your local executive board, president, former trustee, or financial officer.

Questions to Answer before You Begin Your Audit

☐ Have the LM-2 or LM-3 form as well as the IRS 990 forms been filed for the past fiscal year? You may want to inspect a copy of each.

☐ Is the bonding certificate current, and are the necessary individuals covered (you may have a "blanket" bond that covers all officers and stewards)? You may also want to ask whether the amount covered (10 percent of the money handled) is adequate.

☐ Have all financial records necessary to prepare the most recent LM-2 or LM-3 been retained for a minimum of five (5) years?

☐ Based upon an inspection of your constitution and bylaws, what rights and responsibilities, forms, procedures, and deadlines are you required to follow in your audit?

Exercises for Chapter 2

For questions 1–4 below, circle "True" or "False" in response to the statement. For questions 5 and 6, circle the answer you feel is most correct.

1. The rights and responsibilities of union trustees can be found *only* in the Landrum-Griffin Act.

True **False**

2. According to the LMRDA, trustees always have the authority to co-sign checks and loans for their local union.

True **False**

3. Regardless of their union's constitution and bylaws, members can direct their trustees to audit union books at any time.

True **False**

4. Trustees have a responsibility to see that union moneys are used solely for the benefit of the members.

True **False**

5. If any discrepancies are found in local union financial records during the audit, they should first be reported to:

a. the local union's financial officer
b. at the membership meeting
c. the U.S. Department of Labor
d. b and c above
e. all of the above

6. If your financial officer refuses to show you a part of the books or records you need for your audit, what should you do?

a. notify the U.S. Department of Labor
b. file NLRB charges
c. contact the international union
d. continue your investigation anyway
e. notify your executive board

3

Reviewing Income Sources

This chapter reviews the sources of union income and how to verify them during an audit. The union trustee or auditor's goal is to be absolutely certain the union is taking in all the income it is entitled to and to ensure that all sources of income are properly accounted for. Several sample worksheets and forms are provided to assist you in this task, as well as a review of some basic terminology and tools. The final worksheet provides you with a means to summarize your investigation and combine the results of the other worksheets. The chapter concludes with an exercise in which you will apply these tools and worksheets.

Every national and international union has its own unique method of tracking and reporting dues and other income. If there is any conflict between what follows and what your national or international union requires, you should follow your union's own procedure. This is particularly important when it comes to per capita dues reporting. You may be able to adapt the forms and procedures found in this chapter as long as they do not conflict with your union's.

Figure 3–1
Typical Sources of Income of a Local Union

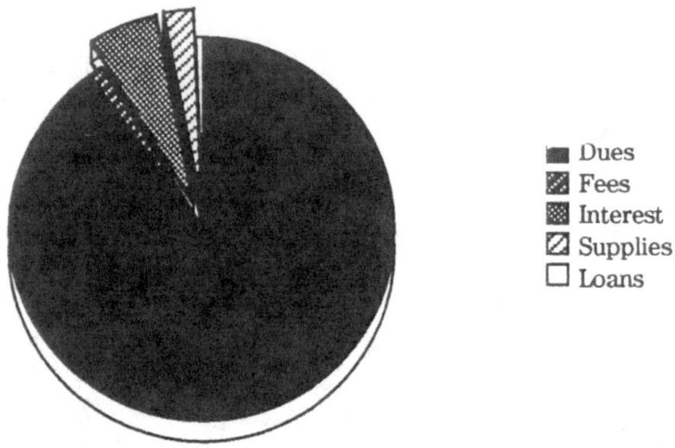

Figure 3–1 illustrates the various sources of income of a local union. Not every local union will have sources identical to those on the chart, but in almost every union membership dues will be the chief source of income. Other possible income sources include:

- ☐ fees and assessments;
- ☐ fines;
- ☐ sales of union supplies (e.g., hats and jackets);
- ☐ rent of office or building space;
- ☐ vending machine sales;
- ☐ loan repayments;
- ☐ interest and dividends; and
- ☐ sales of fixed assets or investments.

The Audit Trail

When income comes into the local union, it should be recorded in the local union's *cash journal* or ledger (fig. 3–2). The cash journal records the *date* the income was received, *who* it was received from, and *the amount* received. In figure 3–2, the amount received is entered in the column that corresponds most closely to the category or account that describes the income source. There may be as few as five or six such categories, or as many as two dozen or more, depending on your local union's journal. It is customary for local unions to obtain cash journal forms from their international or national unions.

Income received is typically entered under *only one income category*. An exception would be a single check that was written for both dues and a fine, initiation fee, or assessment. In this case, *two* or more entries would be made.

Regardless of the forms or recordkeeping system used, there is a basic process or *audit trail* along which all income must travel from the time it is received by the local union until it is put in the bank. This process involves five basic steps (see fig. 3–3).

First, the money is received by a bookkeeper, the financial officer, or someone else in the local union. The money may be received as cash or as a check. It may be self-payment of dues or an employer check for the payroll deduction of dues; it may be from sales of union jackets or hats, vending machine proceeds, the repayment of a loan, or rent charged for use of the union hall for a wedding reception.

Second, the payer should be issued a receipt. This is common practice in the case of individual dues payers and sales of union supplies but is not always done for receipt of employer payroll deductions of dues. The issuance of a receipt establishes *proof* of payment received, both for the payer and the payee. It also establishes a *trail* for the local union auditor or trustee to follow.

Third, the payment should be entered in the union's cash journal. The amount shown on the receipt should equal the amount entered in the cash journal, which must also equal the amount of money actually received. The receipt acts as a check on the cash journal entry; we can verify that the cash journal entry is correct from the receipt and vice versa.

Figure 3–2
Sample Cash Journal Entries

Date	Rec. #	From	Dues	Fees	Sales	Other	Total
3/1/92	1239	V. William	25.50				25.50
3/1/92	1240	J. F. Handle		25.50			25.50
3/1/92	1241	Ace Vending			169.85		169.85
3/3/92	1242	Master Mfg.	1,869.55				1,869.55
3/3/92	1243	J. Brahms			23.25		23.25
3/10/92	1244	E. Wilson				100.00	100.00
3/10/92	1245	S. Vaughan				150.00	150.00
3/22/92	1246	J. Cale		25.00			25.00
3/25/92	1247	West Wood	2,979.25				2,979.25
3/30/92	1248	S. Samson	25.00				25.00
3/30/92	1249	B. Kaufman	51.00				51.00
Totals			4,950.30	50.50	193.10	250.00	5,443.90

Fourth, the check or money should be deposited in the union's bank account. This may not happen every day, but normally it should happen whenever there are sufficient funds to make up a deposit. If all receipts are deposited in the bank, which is the usual procedure, then the amount(s) deposited should equal the amount(s) entered in the cash book, which should equal the amount(s) shown on the receipts, which we know equals the amount of money actually received. To establish an audit trail and prove the money was actually deposited in the bank, you will need a receipt (or deposit slip) from the bank. A deposit slip is also valuable in clearing up questions about how much money was actually deposited (bank tellers sometimes key in the wrong amount on their machines or computers, and the deposit slip is proof of how much was deposited).

Figure 3–3
Audit Trail for Income Received

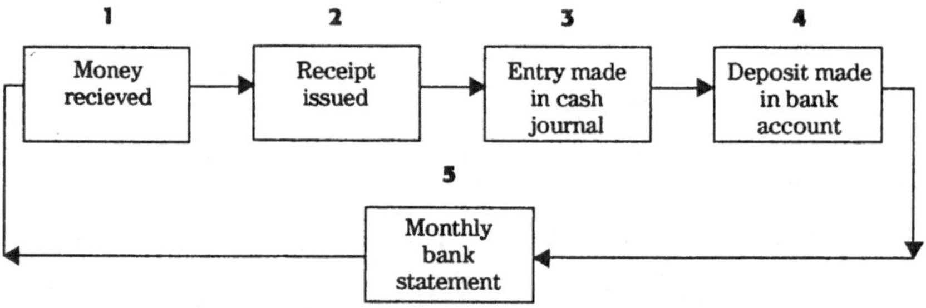

Fifth, and finally, the bank sends the local union a statement of the account. Whether it is a checking account or a savings account, a history of deposits will be listed on the statement. The total of the deposits for the month should equal the total of the deposit slips for the month, the total of cash journal entries for the month, the total of receipts for the month, and the actual money received.

An exception to this rule occurs if the deposits are not posted until the next business day and this falls in the next month or deposits are made in the following month. But over the course of a year, this should all balance out.

The above procedure may seem very simple, but it is important because it creates a *trail* that can be followed. It enables a trustee to compare the totals of receipt slips, deposit slips, and the entries in the cash journal for the same period. As long as each of these totals match, you can be assured that all funds received have been properly accounted for and deposited. This assumes, of course, that receipts were properly issued in the first place.

What information should I request about income for the audit period?

- ☐ **receipt books;**
- ☐ **cash book** or journal;
- ☐ **deposit slips; and**
- ☐ **bank statements.**

Figure 3–4
Receipts and Deposits Worksheet

Audit period starting date:_______________ Ending date:_______________

1. Add up the *cash journal* entries from the starting to the ending dates and enter the total here. $_______________

2. Add up the receipts from the *receipt book* from the starting to the ending dates and enter the total here. $_______________

3. Are receipts *always* written for every payment received by the local union? Yes___ No___ $_______________
If "no," go to question 5.

4. Subtract the figure in line 2 from the figure in line 1 and enter the amount here. $_______________

5. Add up *all deposit slips* from the starting to the ending dates and enter the total here. $_______________

6. Are all deposit slips saved for the audit period?
Yes___ No___ *If "no," go to question 9.* $_______________

7. Add up *all* the deposits from the *bank statements* which fall between the beginning and ending dates of the audit period and enter the total here. $_______________

8. Subtract the figure in line 7 from the figure in line 5 and enter the result here. $_______________

9. Subtract the figure in line 7 from the figure in line 1 and enter the total here. $_______________

10. Is the figure in line 9 zero? Yes___ No___

If "yes" and the answers to questions 3 and 6 were "yes," go to question 11. If "no," there may be discrepancies in cash journal entries and/or deposits.

11. Is the figure in line 4 zero? Yes___ No___

If "yes," your cash journal receipts equal the receipts issued to payers. If "no" and the answer to question 3 was "yes," you should check each receipt against each cash book entry and recheck your addition.

12. Is the figure in line 8 zero? Yes___ No___

If "yes" and the answer to question 6 is "yes," the total on your deposit slips equals your bank deposit (no bank errors). If "no" and the answer to question 6 is "yes," you should check each deposit slip against each monthly statement and each cash journal record to find discrepancies.

The worksheet in figure 3-4 can be used to make sure that documentation of all receipts and deposits is adequate for the audit period.

In effect, what we are doing here is making sure that our records of the union's income correspond to the deposit records of the bank, much as we do when we reconcile our own personal checkbook each month to see whether our bank balance jibes with our checkbook balance.

Now let's take a closer look at each of the income sources listed above. For each source, we will review the audit trail that is created and how to follow this trail to make sure all income owed has been received and properly accounted for.

Dues

Local union dues may be collected through *payroll deductions* or by *self-payment*. In the case of self-payment, dues may be paid monthly, quarterly, or semi-annually, depending on local bylaws. Most local union dues include the per capita tax to the national or international union, district or regional councils, or state or central labor bodies. In some unions, per capita payments are treated as a source of income separate from local union dues.

There is considerable variety in the dues that are charged and in how the per capita tax is passed on to parent organizations or affiliates. Nonetheless, two basic principles apply to all dues collection and recordkeeping from the local union trustees' point of view:

☐ In the case of payroll deductions, the dues collected must jibe with the payroll list furnished by the employer. In other words, if local union dues are $20 per month and there are 550 members, the payroll deduction check must equal $20 x 550 or $11,000, *and* the payroll records list furnished by the employer should indicate that there were 550 eligible dues payers for the period.

☐ The amount of dues *owed* by members (whether through payroll deductions or self-payment) should be verified from union membership records, such as dues cards, ledgers, or rosters. The amount *owed* each month or payment period must equal the amount actually *collected*.

These rules should be self-explanatory. Local union auditors and trustees need to be certain that every penny in dues owed is actually collected, deposited, and accounted for and that adequate records are kept. In large locals, it may be necessary to take a *random sample* of all self-payers. In this case, you would start with a list of all self-payers and randomly pick 30 percent of them (or simply pick every third one off the list). You would then go back through their dues records to determine what dues they *owed* for the audit period and then through the cash journal and receipt books to determine what dues they actually *paid* for the same period. The amount owed and the amount paid for each of these randomly selected members should be equal. Remember, if you use the random sample method, you must clearly state this in your audit report.

What records should I ask for to review income from dues?

☐ Copies of all receipts issued to self-payers;

☐ printouts or rosters that accompany the payroll deduction checks sent by the employers;

☐ pages from the cash journal; and

☐ dues cards or rosters to establish the amount of dues actually owed.

This job may seem tedious, but remember that dues are the largest source of union income. You and your members want to be absolutely certain that every member is paying his or her fair share—nothing more and nothing less. Moreover, in the case of payroll deductions, you want to be certain that the employer is correctly deducting dues from the paycheck of every member of the bargaining unit who is eligible. Figures 3–5 and 3–6 provide worksheets to help you audit dues income for your local union.

The worksheet in figure 3–5 can be used for one month at a time, for the entire audit period, or, if you use a random sample (as described above) of self-payers, for each individual self-payer.

Figure 3–6 is a worksheet for payroll deduction dues income. Before auditing payroll deduction dues income, you will need to decide how extensive a check of records you want to do. This will depend in large part on the number of employers who send in dues and the number of members on each deduction list. In large locals, you may want to do only *one* such test; in other words, pick one payroll period for one employer, and then use the worksheet and procedure below to determine whether or not the correct amount of dues owed was actually collected. In very small local unions, you may wish to do this for all employers and all payroll periods during the audit period.

Figure 3–5
Self-Paid Dues Worksheet

Audit period starting date:_______________ Ending date:_______________

1. From local union records, list the *number* of self-paying members for the audit period. _______________

2. Multiply the number of self-payers times the number of pay periods included in the audit period times the dues amount per person for each pay period.

_______________	x	_______________	x	$_______________
no. of self-payers		no. of pay periods		dues amount/pay period

= $_______________**Total self-paid dues owed**

3. From the cash journal for the audit period, list the name, date, amount paid, and receipt number for each self-payment (use additional sheets if necessary, but enter the total amount paid below).

Date paid	*Name*	*Amount paid*	*Receipt #*

Total self-paid dues collected for the period: $_______________

4. Go through the receipt books for the audit period and place a check mark next to each entry listed in question 3 above for which you have a receipt.

Do you have receipts for all entries in question 3 above?

Yes_____ No_____

You may not have issued receipts to all self-payers if the number of receipts is less than the number of entries in question 3 above. You may have failed to enter all self-payments in the cash journal if the number of receipts is greater than the number of entries. In either case, check with the local union's financial officer for further explanation.

5. Compare the total of self-paid dues *collected* (question 3) with the amount of self-paid dues *owed*. **Are the two amounts equal?** Yes_____ No_____

If the answer is "yes," you have collected the proper amount of self-paid dues. If the figure in question 3 is greater than the figure in question 2, some members may have overpaid their dues, or not all entries have been made in the cash journal.

If the figure in question 2 is greater than the figure in question 3, then you have not collected enough dues from self-payers, or some self-payers may not have paid their dues at all. Either discrepancy should be investigated immediately.

Figure 3–6
Payroll Deduction of Dues (PRD) Worksheet

Month or pay period:________________ Employer:________________

Item	*Members*	*Dues owed*		*Amount($)*
1. Number of PRD dues payers from *previous* pay period:	______	$______	=	$______
2. New members since *previous* pay period (include recalls/reinstatements):	______	$______	=	$______
3. Exceptions since *previous* pay period (layoffs, quits, leaves, or disabilities):	______	$______	=	$______
4. Subtotal (add lines 1 and 2 then subtract line 3):	______	$______	=	$______
5. From the payroll list or listing provided with the *current* PRD check, enter the number of members and the total dues enclosed.	______	$______	=	$______
6. Subtract line 5 from line 4.	______	$______	=	$______

If line 6 is a negative number (less than zero), the employer may have *overpaid* dues for the month. This may be because the employer had incorrect information regarding the working status of certain members. You should attempt to reconcile these differences as soon as possible.

If line 6 is a positive number (dues owed is greater than dues collected), the employer may not have deducted *enough* dues. You should try to verify the differences and reconcile them with the employer.

Regardless of your decision, you can use the worksheet in figure 3–6. It is designed to cover *one* payroll period *per* employer, but it can be used many times. If you decide to do one or two pay periods, you should pick the months of the year when the greatest potential difference between the amount owed and the amount collected is likely to exist. This may be summer vacation months or deer hunting season, because people on vacation may not have the correct dues being deducted. If the employer has deducted the correct amount of dues (the dues actually owed) for these months, it is more likely that the employer has handled dues deduction properly for the rest of the audit period.

If you find an over- or underpayment, you should bring it to the attention of your financial officer immediately.

Fees and Assessments

Fees here means *initiation* fees that all new members must pay, unless waived or reduced in accordance with the union's constitution and bylaws. Assessments typically include special one-time payments members must pay for extraordinary items, such as defense funds or legal fees.

Before you begin the audit of fees and assessments, you should obtain a list of new members or their membership cards for the audit period. There may be a similar form for reinstatements. If so, you should request this as well. You should also review the cash journal and the receipt book to make sure a receipt has been issued for each initiation fee and for assessments that were self-paid.

The procedure used here is similar to the one used for dues. First, obtain a list of members who *owe* initiation fees for the audit period. Next, using the cash book or receipts, determine the amount actually *collected* from these individuals. Finally, compare the two figures, which should be equal. Figure 3–7 can be used for this purpose. A separate worksheet should be filled out for fees and for assessments.

In the case of special assessments, the audit procedure may be more difficult. Your first job will be to obtain a list of all members who are subject to the assessment. *This may not be the entire membership, depending on the terms of the assessment resolution*. The next task is to gather all the receipts for payment of this assessment. You should be looking for the following:

Figure 3–7
Fees, Fines, and Assessments Worksheet

Audit period starting date:________________ Ending date:________________

This worksheet is being used for (check one):

Initiation fees _____ Fines _____ Special assessments_____

You should use this worksheet for only one of the above purposes. Do not use it for more than one purpose; fill out a separate worksheet instead.

1. From local union records, list the *number* of new members (eligible members) for the audit period who paid initiation fees (assessments or fines).

2. Multiply the number of (new) members times the initiation fee (fine or assessment amount)

________________ x $ ____________________ = $____________**total owed**
no. of new members fee, assessment, or fine amount

3. From the cash journal for the audit period, list the name, date, amount paid and receipt number issued for each payment (use extra sheets if necessary, but show total collected below).

Date paid *Name* *Amount paid* *Receipt #*

Total *collected* for the period: $________________

4. Go through the receipt books for the audit period and place a check mark next to each entry in question 3 above for which you have a receipt.

Do you have receipts for all entries in question 3 above?

Yes___ No___

If the answer is "no," you need to reconcile the difference. You may not have issued receipts to all individuals if the number of receipts is less than the number of entries in question 3 above. You may have failed to enter all payments in the cash journal if the number of receipts is greater than the number of entries. In either case, check with the local union's financial officer for further explanation.

5. Compare the total of payments *collected* (line 3) with the amount of payments *owed* (line 2).

Are the two amounts equal? Yes___No___

If the answer to question 5 is "yes," you have collected the proper amount of payments owed. If line 3 is greater than line 2, some members may have overpaid,or not all entries have been made in the cash journal.

If line 2 is greater than line 3, then you have not collected enough from members, or some may not have paid at all. Either discrepancy should be investigated immediately.

☐ Does the number of members subject to the assessment *equal* the number for whom you actually have payment receipts?

☐ Does the number of payment receipts times the amount of the assessment equal the amount collected?

If there are any discrepancies, you should bring them to the attention of your local union financial officer immediately. Possible exceptions include partial payment of assessments, waivers of assessments for hardship cases by executive board action, or appeals of assessment payments filed properly and on time.

Fines

Unions normally have the right to fine members for violations of the union constitution, bylaws, and policies. When such fines are levied and collected, a receipt should be issued to the member and a copy of the receipt kept. The amount of the fine should be recorded in the cash journal. In auditing your records, you should obtain a list of members who were assessed fines during the audit period or who had outstanding fines from previous audit periods. The names of each of these members and the fines associated with each should be listed and this list checked against both the cash journal and the receipt book. Fines may not be collected if a member has filed an appeal or the local union has decided not to pursue a collection action in court. These decisions and appeals should be documented in minutes of the executive board or local union meetings.

You may use the worksheet in figure 3–7 for reviewing fines.

Sales of Union Supplies

The sale of union supplies is an area in which sloppy recordkeeping can cost the local union money. Hats and jackets with the union logo are a popular item in many local unions and are often given away as door prizes or at awards ceremonies. If these items are purchased as gifts or awards and are not for sale, then a sale is obviously not intended, and this section of the chapter will not apply. If the supplies are purchased with union political action funds with the intent to raise political contributions, this section will not apply, since political action funds are normally segregated from union funds. Your union should have instructions for recordkeeping involving political action funds.

Figure 3–8
Sale of Union Supplies Worksheet

Audit period starting date:______________ Ending date:______________

1. Inventory at *beginning* of period:

Item	*Quantity*	*Unit sales price*	*Subtotal*

Totals:

2. Inventory acquired *during* audit period:

Item	*Quantity*	*Unit sales price*	*Subtotal*

Totals:

3. Inventory at *end* of audit period:

Item	*Quantity*	*Unit sales price*	*Subtotal*

Totals:

4. *Sales of supplies* during audit period (enter these from the cash journal records for the period):

Item	*Quantity*	*Unit sales price*	*Subtotal*

Totals:

You should also check your receipts book to make sure you have issued a receipt for each sale. For every receipt you have, place a check in the far right column above.

5. Add the total value in line 1 (inventory at beginning of period) plus the total value in line 2 (inventory added during audit period) and subtract the total value of line 4 (sales of supplies during audit period).

Enter amount here: $_________

Does this value equal the total value in line 3 (inventory at the end of the audit period)? Yes_____ No_____

If the answer is "yes," then you have properly accounted for all inventory items, sales, and other transactions for the audit period. If the answer is "no", you have not accounted for all sales (check your receipts), additions, or your beginning or ending inventory was incomplete. You should attempt to reconcile these differences.

If the local union purchases union supplies for the purpose of selling them and putting the proceeds of the sale in the local union treasury, every hat, jacket, pen and pencil set, T-shirt and belt buckle the local union has purchased for this purpose should be included in an inventory. An inventory of all such supplies should be prepared at the end of every audit period. This inventory should then be compared with the one for the previous period to determine which items are no longer in inventory. Items no longer in inventory should then be multiplied by their sales price and summed up. This total should equal the total of all sales of union supplies for the period, which can be verified from receipt books or cash journals, adjusted for any new acquisitions. Receipts should be issued for each sale, and the sum of the sales receipts should equal the amount purchased during the audit period. Figure 3–8 is a worksheet you can use for this purpose. If there are discrepancies, the individual in charge of the union supplies inventory (usually the financial officer of the local union) should be contacted for an explanation.

Rental of Office or Building Space

Unions that own their hall often rent out office space or meeting rooms to other union or fraternal organizations, as well as to the general public for receptions, meetings, or other gatherings. It is recommended that the union draw up a standard lease contract or agreement that spells out the terms of any long-term lease of space. A contract may even be wise for evening rentals of the hall. A standard fee schedule also makes review of the rents received much easier.

A receipt should be issued for each and every rental payment collected, and the amount of the receipt should be entered in the cash journal. A log of all space rentals for the audit period should also be kept, and the receipts compared against this log to ensure that all payments were made properly and in a timely manner. Figure 3–9 is a suggested worksheet for this income source.

Vending Machine Sales

Many local unions enter into agreements with vending machine companies to sell soda, candy, or other products in the union building or office space. While the details of these contracts vary, most local unions receive some percentage of the total sales. This is considered income. A receipt should be issued to the vending machine company for each payment and this amount entered in the cash journal.

Figure 3–9
Rental Income Worksheet

Audit period starting date:______________ Ending date:______________

1. From local union records such as a log or calendar of rental space, list all rentals for the audit period for which payment was charged and/or received.

Party renting space	*Date(s) of rental*	*Amount charged ($)*

Total rent *owed:* $__________

2. From the cash journal for the audit period, list all rental payments received. If receipts for payments are used, you should place a check mark in the far right-hand column for each rental payment recorded in the cash journal.

Party renting space	*Date(s) of rental*	*Amount charged ($)*	*Receipt issued?*

Total rent *collected*: $__________

3. Subtract line 2 (rent collected) from line 1 (rent owed). $__________

4. If line 3 is zero, all rent payments are properly accounted for.

If line 3 is negative (rent collected is greater than rent owed), there may be some overpayment or failure to enter rent payments in the journal.

If line 3 is positive (rent owed exceeds rent collected), not all collections may have been entered or some additional rent may be owed.

You should be certain that the total of the receipts issued equals the total of the vending machine sales entries in the journal for the audit period. If there are discrepancies, these should be investigated. You may also wish to check the terms of the vending machine contract to make certain that the payments are being made properly and on time.

Loan Repayments

In some cases, local unions make loans to individual members, their families, or local businesses. Many international and national unions, however, urge their local unions *not* to make loans to *anybody*. You should clarify your union's policy. If you find during your audit that loans have been made in violation of this policy, you should report this to your financial officer immediately.

Such loans must not place the local union in any conflict of interest and must meet the other fiduciary standards spelled out in the union constitution and bylaws as well as in Section 501(a) of the Landrum-Griffin Act. Normally, loans must involve a note that spells out the collateral, the principal of the loan, the interest rate, and the repayment schedule, as well as the penalties for failure to comply. Standard forms for loan agreements can be purchased at most bookstores.

In reviewing loan payments made to the local, you should obtain the following:

- ☐ a copy of all outstanding loan notes or contracts, which will include the loan repayment schedule; and
- ☐ a copy of all receipts for loan repayments made during the period of the audit.

You will need to check that all loan repayments have been made according to schedule and that each receipt has been recorded in the cash journal. If payments have not been made on time, you should confer with the local union's financial officer for an explanation. You can use the worksheet in figure 3–10 to help you.

Sales of Fixed Assets or Investments

Over the course of the period being audited, the local union may have an opportunity to sell off fixed assets, such as stock, bonds, furniture, office equipment, or property. A review of these transactions is both important and in many cases difficult. Further, each sales transaction may involve special circumstances, so trustees must proceed carefully. Several general steps, however, do apply:

Figure 3–10
Loan Repayment Worksheet

1. Using union files and other records, including the note or loan contract, list for each loan the number of installments due during the audit period and the total amount of the payments due during this period.

Who was loan made to?	*Number of repayment installments due*	*Total amount due during period*

Total amount from loan payments due during period: $____________

2. From the cash journal for the audit period, list for *each loan* the loan payments *actually* received, the amount received, and if receipts were issued to the payee. Check the far right column if you have a copy of a receipt for each payment received.

Payee	*Date of payment*	*Amount of payment*	*Was receipt issued?*

Total loans repaid during period: $____________

3. Subtract the total in line 1 (loans due) from line 2 (loans paid) and enter the result here. $____________

4. If the total in line 3 is zero, all loans due during the period have been paid. If the number is not zero, there may be over- or underpayments, and this will require closer scrutiny of the note or loan contract, cash journal, and receipt records.

Figure 3–11
Income Worksheet

Audit period starting date:________________ Ending date:________________

Enter the cash journal totals for the audit period for each of the items below. If, in filling out the preceding worksheets, your amounts owed did not equal your amounts collected, put an asterisk (*) by this item to indicate that you were not able to adequately reconcile these income sources with available records. This will require follow-up action.

1. Dues
  a. Self-paid dues (fig. 3–5): __________
  b. Payroll deduction dues (fig. 3–6): __________
  c. Subtotal—dues (a plus b) __________

2. Fees and Assessments (fig. 3–7): __________

3. Fines (fig. 3–7): __________

4. Sale of Union Supplies (fig. 3–8): __________

5. Rent (fig. 3–9): __________

6. Vending Machine Sales (total sales): __________

7. Loan Repayments (fig. 3–10): __________

8. Other Income (amounts not included in worksheets): __________

9. Grand Total: __________

10. Grand total of deposit slips: __________

11. Subtract line 10 (total deposits) from line 9 (Grand total). __________

12. Does line 11 equal zero? Yes____ No____

- ☐ Obtain a copy of the original purchase order or invoice that states the purchase price of the asset. This could be a bill of sale for office equipment, furniture, or an automobile. In the case of property, it could be the mortgage, deed, sales contract, or other related document.

- ☐ Try, if possible, to obtain an estimate of the worth of the asset at the time of the sale. This may be difficult, particularly with equipment or furniture that has outlived its useful service life. This is one advantage of using a depreciation schedule (see chap. 4 for more information). In the case of automobiles, a Blue Book estimate will sometimes be sufficient. Investments can present even more difficulty, because investments may have a book value and a market value. Property (land and buildings) may also have an assessed value and a market value.

- ☐ Compare the sale price with the estimated value of the asset and the purchase price. In many cases, the sale price will have been approved by the executive board, so you may wish to refer to the minutes for guidance.

- ☐ Finally, compare the sale price from the contract with the entry made in the cash journal to be certain they are identical. If not, you may need to seek further explanation from the union's financial officer.

Putting It All Together

The final step of your income audit is to determine whether the cash journal totals for the period balance with the total deposits made to the bank. In other words, you need to be sure that every penny collected and recorded has been properly deposited in the union's checking or savings accounts. Figure 3–11 provides a worksheet for this purpose (fig. 3–4 is used to make sure adequate documentation of all receipts is available; fig. 3–11 is a summary worksheet that incorporates information from all the worksheets in this chapter).

Finally, if you have verified that receipts exist for every cash journal entry, then line 12 in figure 3–11 will equal zero. If line 12 is not zero, it means that either you don't have receipts for every entry, or the income amount on the receipt may differ from that in the cash journal. These discrepancies should be identified and brought to the attention of the local union financial officer.

Figure 3–11 is a good summary. You may wish to include it in your final report to the union executive board or general membership body.

Exercises for Chapter 3

1. Your self-paid dues worksheet (see fig. 3–5) provides the following information: Total owed $2,497.50
Total collected $2,442.50

Monthly dues for the audit period are $18.50 per month.

Answer the following:

a. What do you think is wrong?
b. What might have caused this to happen?
c. What do you think needs to be done?

2. Your monthly payroll deduction worksheet (fig. 3–6) reveals the following information (monthly dues are $23.25):

Item	*Members*	*Amount ($)*
Number of PRD dues payers from previous pay period	515	11,973.75
New members	24	558.00
Exceptions	15	348.75
Subtotal	524	12,183.00
PRD collected	514	11,950.50
Subtotal minus collected	10	232.50

Answer the following:

a. What do you think is wrong?
b. What might have caused this to happen?
c. What do you think needs to be done?

3. Your fees, fines, and assessment worksheet (fig. 3–7) for 1989–90 indicates you have collected $1,700 and that $1,600 was actually owed.

Answer the following:

a. What do you think is wrong?
b. What might have caused this to happen?
c. What do you think needs to be done?

4. Completing your rental income worksheet (fig. 3–9), you find the amount of rent owed was $1,458.96 and the amount collected was $1,278.96.

Answer the following:

a. What do you think is wrong?
b. What might have caused this to happen?
c. What do you think needs to be done?

4
Union Assets

Most union officers or trustees give little thought to local union *assets*. After all, local unions are not generally very complex organizations in financial terms. Assets can be defined here as the sum of the value of all property held by the union that can be used to offset financial liabilities. Local unions have both *liquid* and *fixed* assets. Liquid assets, those which can be easily converted into cash, include checking and savings accounts, certificates of deposit, stocks, and bonds. Fixed assets, those that *cannot* be easily converted into cash, include property, buildings, automobiles, furniture, and office equipment. These assets belong to the union and therefore must be held "for the exclusive benefit of the union and its members."

Responsibilities of Union Trustees

When it comes to managing assets, trustees have several responsibilities, including but not necessarily limited to the following:

- ☐ Verifying that signatories of liquid assets (checking and savings accounts, certificates of deposits, etc.) are current. Election of new officers require that signature cards, titles, and addresses be updated.

- ☐ Verifying that adequate records are available to establish the disposition of assets and their value. This involves inspecting stock and bond certificates, automobile records, and insurance certificates to be certain that autos, property, and other valuables are properly insured.

- ☐ Verifying that liquid asset transactions such as purchases, reinvestments, and rollovers are properly managed. Trustees need to make sure that investments that mature are rolled over or transferred in accordance with the local union's authorization, and that interest and dividends are paid in the proper amount and on time.

☐ Making sure that inventories of office furniture and equipment are kept current.

☐ If the union property is depreciated, making sure that assets are depreciated according to a schedule.

Each of the above areas of responsibility is discussed in more detail below with examples and check lists. Additional responsibilities may be appropriate, depending on the assets owned by your local union. For example, if the local union owns automobiles for officer and staff use, it may be necessary to review vehicle records and mileage logs. Because this situation applies to relatively few local unions, this topic is not discussed in this chapter. Check with your international or national union for forms or suggestions for dealing with automobile use and other assets.

At the end of this chapter is an exercise in which you can apply some of these principles to real-life situations.

What information should I ask for in order to determine the status and value of union assets?

☐ Copies of all certificates of deposit, contracts for money market funds, stock and bond certificates, and investment documents.

☐ Copies of signature cards for any account on which an officer or employee of the local union can draw money (CDs, money market funds, checking and savings accounts).

☐ If the local union owns property or vehicles, copies of the titles, mortgage or loan contracts, and insurance contracts and tax assessment on property.

☐ Equipment and furniture inventories.

Verifying Signatories

Whenever there is a turnover of union officers, signature cards for checking and savings accounts and other asset ownership papers need to be updated.

Signature cards are usually filed with the bank or financial institution holding the account. You may request copies of these cards, and, if changes are required, copy the revised cards so that you will have them on file the next time you need to verify this information. All the signature cards should be compared with the list of *currently authorized* signatories. You may use the worksheet in figure 4–1 for this purpose. If signature cards need to be updated because of changes in officers, notify your financial officer immediately.

Figure 4–1
Signatories Worksheet

Audit Period Starting Date:_______________ Ending Date:_______________

1. List all *currently authorized* signatories.

2. For each account or asset for which signatures of officers may be required, list those names on the most recent signature card.

Asset name	*Account #*	*Authorized signatories*

3. Check to see that the address listed on the signature card and on all account statements is the correct mailing address for the local union.

Are all addresses correct? Yes_____ No_____

If some accounts or assets do not have up-to-date signatories, you should immediately bring this to the attention of the local union financial officer and ask that it be corrected.

Verifying Records

Making certain that adequate records are available to establish the disposition of all assets is a relatively simple yet important task for trustees. Because of turnover in union offices, there may be good recordkeepers followed by bad recordkeepers, individuals who carefully save everything, and others who save nothing. Just because you have a signature card for an account at the bank, a stock certificate, or a money market fund contract does *not* mean that the account is still active or that it even has funds in it! At the same time, if there are *no* records for you to verify the existence of a liquid asset, you have no way of even knowing of its existence!

For this reason, it is important that you ask your local union financial officer for records of *all* the liquid assets the union owns including checking and savings accounts, money market funds, certificates of deposit, stocks, and bonds. If the list is incomplete, you may have to contact banks, brokers, or credit unions directly. You will need to see some statement for each and every one of these so you can verify that they are active. These records can tell you the current value of each account.

If your review reveals that there is no statement for an account that was active in a previous audit, you may wish to have the financial secretary-treasurer contact the bank, broker, or credit union to determine the status of the account and to obtain a current statement. Never treat an account as closed until you have a statement from the bank, broker, or credit union clearly indicating that the account is closed.

Verifying Asset Transactions

Trustees need to verify that all asset transactions handled by third parties such as banks, brokers, or money market managers have been done in a timely manner and in accordance with any contracts and union authorization. Make certain you have requested the information detailed on page 40.

Many international and national unions recommend that a local union *not* purchase more than a single share of a stock of companies with whom the local union has a collective bargaining agreement. If you have any doubts regarding this policy, check with your local union financial officer or international union.

Interest-Bearing Checking and Savings Accounts

Have all interest payments been posted to the account in a timely manner? To answer this, you must know whether interest is paid monthly, quarterly, or semi-annually. Interest should be posted by a certain date and show up in the statement of account. A telephone call to the bank or credit union can usually clear up any questions or misunderstandings.

Certificates of Deposit

Certificates of deposits pay a specified rate of interest over a specific term, and when the certificate *matures* (the ending date is reached), the bank or institution that holds the certificate usually gives the holder an opportunity either to withdraw the balance or to "roll over" the amount. In the latter case, it would simply sit and earn interest for another term. In many cases, the bank or institution simply notifies the customer that the certificate will automatically roll over for another term unless it hears otherwise by a certain date. These notices should be examined to make certain that adequate notice is given to the union of the maturity date. The decision to roll over a certificate of deposit or to withdraw it will normally require executive board action.

Money Market Funds

Unlike certificates of deposit, money market funds normally pay a variable rate of interest for a specified period of time. You should be certain that dividends are paid by the date specified in the contract and that only the administrative fee specified is charged. Questions regarding posting of dividends to the account or administrative fees should be directed first to the local union financial officer.

Stocks and Bonds

Stocks and bonds are normally purchased and sold through a broker, who will charge a commission. A statement of account is usually provided on a regular basis. You should review these statements carefully to determine what stocks and bonds are owned, what their market or book value is, and whether or not the broker is charging a proper commission. This review will normally require that you read any brokerage agreements. You should not hesitate to ask the local union's financial officer if you have questions.

You can use the figure 4–2 worksheet to record any questions, apparent problems or discrepancies, as well as any checks that you make relative to each liquid asset.

Figure 4–2
Asset Transaction Worksheet

Audit period starting date:_______________ Ending date:_______________

1. Savings and checking accounts (interest)

   Have interest payments to each account been posted properly and on time?

   Yes_____ No_____

2. Certificates of deposit

   Have interest payments been posted to the account properly and on time?

   Yes_____ No_____

   Has proper and timely notice of the maturity date been received?

   Yes_____ No_____

3. Money market funds

   Have all dividend payments been posted to the account properly and on time?

   Yes_____ No_____

   Has the proper administrative or service fee been charged?

   Yes_____ No_____

4. Stocks and bonds

   List the number of shares of stock or bonds held at the *beginning* and *end* of the audit period, the book value of each, whether or not a brokerage fee was charged, and whether it was the proper charge.

5. Were there any discrepancies or problems?

Maintaining Inventory Records

Keeping an inventory of all of the local union's fixed assets, such as office equipment and furniture, is an important safeguard. It helps keep track of what the union does and does not own and provides documentation for when equipment or furniture needs to be replaced. Inventories do not have to be very complicated. A sample form for an inventory of office equipment and furniture is provided in figure 4–3. This inventory should be updated annually. If fixed assets are not depreciated, the "accumulated depreciation" column may be deleted. Some local unions will use the original cost of the item as the book value, and others will "expense" the value of each asset. Check with your local financial officer or international or national union for details.

Figure 4–3
Sample Inventory Form

Audit period starting date:________________ Ending date:________________

Item	Date Purchased	Cost	Accumulated Depreciation	Book Value

List any items that were on the last period's worksheet but that are not on this worksheet, with an explanation why.

Item *Explanation*

List any items that are on this worksheet but that were not on the last period's worksheet (such as new acquisitions or purchases).

You will need a copy of the inventory for the *previous* audit period so you can compare it with the one for the present period. This will enable you to verify any changes, such as equipment sold, donated, or missing. Changes should be noted and explained on the worksheet. Missing items should be accounted for and immediately brought to the attention of the local union's financial officer.

Depreciating Assets

As anyone who has traded in an automobile for a new or newer model knows, automobiles do not retain their full value over time. Carrying your fixed assets on your books at their original purchase price ignores the fact that many of these fixed assets will depreciate. In other words, they will lose much of their original value over time. This may result in overstating the value of some of these assets.

Few local unions actually depreciate their fixed assets. There is no real penalty for overstating a local union's fixed assets, or any significant tax advantage, as there is in a for-profit business. The only reason for depreciating fixed assets, besides custom or tradition, is to reflect the value of these assets more accurately.

If you do depreciate fixed assets, you should use a depreciation schedule, such as the one shown in figure 4–4. In this example, we assume a five-year straight-line method for depreciating office equipment and a ten-year straight-line method for depreciating office furniture. In the case of the office equipment, this means that in a five-year period, the fixed asset depreciates at an even rate, or at the same amount each year, and that after five years, it has depreciated to zero value. In the case of the furniture, we are saying that after ten years, the depreciated value is zero. With the five-year method, the asset loses 20 percent of its value each year; with the ten-year method, the asset loses 10 percent of its value each year. A depreciation schedule simply lists what the depreciated value of each fixed asset is each year over its useful life.

Referring to figure 4–4, assume that in 1986 a local union purchases twenty folding chairs for $528.71. In 1989, it purchases a copy machine for $1,475.89, and in 1990, it purchases a computer system for $3,862.25. If we chose not to depreciate these fixed assets, we would carry them on the books at the value of their sales price. But if we were to depreciate these

Figure 4–4
Sample Depreciation Schedule

	Copy Machine	**Computer**	**Folding Chairs**
Year Purchased	1989	1990	1986
Sales Price	1,475.89	3,862.25	528.71
First-Year Value	1,180.71	3,089.80	475.84
Second-Year Value	885.53	2,317.35	422.97
Third-Year Value	590.36	1,544.90	370.10
Fourth-Year Value	295.18	772.45	317.23
Fifth-Year Value	0.00	0.00	264.36

assets, the copy machine and computer would lose 20 percent of their original value each year for five years and the chairs would lose 10 percent of their value each year.

This does not mean that the assets would be worth nothing at the end of the depreciation term. We might be able to sell the computer for several hundred dollars in 1995 and use the copy machine as a trade in on a new model in 1994. We could probably sell our chairs at a rummage sale for a few dollars each in the year 2000.

On the flip side, some fixed assets, such as real estate or property, normally *appreciate* in value over time. That is, they become *more* valuable, not *less* valuable as is the case in depreciation.

The depreciated value of the assets, if depreciation schedules are used, is included on the LM-2 form.

Exercises for Chapter 4

1. Complete the depreciation schedule below, filling in the blank cells marked "a" through "h."

	Telephones	Typewriter	
Year Purchased	1989	1990	
Sales Price	$125.00	$300.00	
First-Year Value	$100.00	$240.00	
Second-Year Value	a	e	
Third-Year Value	b	f	
Fourth-Year Value	c	g	
Fifth-Year Value	d	h	

2. Your review of inventory records for the local union reveals that a telephone answering machine was purchased in 1988 and entered on the inventory in that year and in 1989. But you cannot find it on the inventory for 1990, and there is no record of its sale in the cash journal and there is no receipt. What should you do?

3. A small savings account that was opened ten years ago has been inactive for some time, and you discover a copy of the passbook and signature cards during your audit. No one on the executive board is aware of this account, and the balance is $500. What should you do?

5
Disbursements

Responsibilities of the Trustee

The responsibilities of trustees with regard to disbursements are as follows:

- ☐ to verify that all expenses have been properly *authorized* in accordance with the union's constitution and bylaws;

- ☐ to verify that there is adequate documentation of those expenses on file to demonstrate that those funds were expended for their authorized purpose; and

- ☐ to ensure that all disbursements have been properly accounted for.

The Audit Trail for Disbursements

To carry out these responsibilities, local union trustees and auditors have a definite *audit trail* to follow, not unlike the one described in chapter 3. The audit trail for expenses is detailed in figure 5–1.

The first step of the audit trail for expenses is that the local union's governing body *authorizes* expenditures of union funds. This authorization should occur *before* the funds are spent, not after. The way this authorization is given varies from union to union, depending on each union's constitution and bylaws.

Once an expense has been authorized, a check is normally written on the union's checking account. The check number, date, amount, and payee should be recorded in the checkbook register. Some unions may use petty

Figure 5–1
Overview of Authorization, Documentation, and Disbursement Process

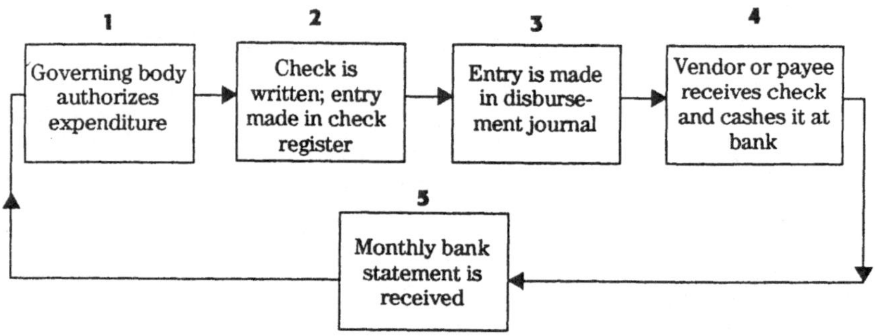

cash funds, but it is recommended that checks be used whenever possible. The check should generally *not* be written until the financial officer receives some form of documentation, a *voucher, receipt, or bill,* that shows that the funds will be spent for the authorized purpose. The types of documentation typically required for various expenses are discussed in more detail below.

At the time the check is written, an entry is usually made in the union's disbursement journal or ledger. The check number, date, and payee are recorded, and the amount is entered in the column of the journal that most closely describes the expense. Figure 5–2 shows a sample disbursement journal. Typically, the amount of the check is recorded in only one column.

Next, the vendor or payee named on the check endorses the check and cashes it at the bank. The endorsement, as well as some identification, are usually required by the bank. Once the check clears the local union's bank, the canceled checks for that month are sent back to the local union with the monthly bank statement. At this time, the financial officer must *reconcile* the bank's account balance with the local union's *book* balance. A sample reconciliation form is found in figure 5–5.

Figure 5–2
Sample Disbursement Journal
Month: November Year: 1990

Date	Check #	Payee	Per Capita Dues	Salary	Fringes	Lost Wages	Taxes	Office/ Admin
11/1/90	1236	Int'l Union	23,650					
11/1/90	1237	President		1,264				
11/2/90	1238	H&W Trust			396			
11/2/90	1239	Fed Tax					322	
11/14/90	1240	State Travel					148	
11/14/90	1241	Steward L.W.				103		
11/15/90	1242	Postage Meter						37
11/15/90	1243	Xerox Paper						43
11/23/90	1244	Ace Printing						124
11/23/90	1245	Steward L.W.				190		
11/23/90	1246	Phone Company						92
11/23/90	1247	V.P. Lost Wages				365		
11/23/90	1248	State AFL-CIO	100					
11/30/90	1249	Labor Council	50					
11/30/90	1250	Utility Company						99
11/30/90	1251	Sec'y Salery		1198				
11/30/90	1252	Sec'y Fringes			346			
Totals			**23,800**	**2,462**	**742**	**658**	**470**	**395**

As is the case with income, each step in this procedure leaves a trail. The authorization typically requires an entry in the minutes of the executive board or local membership; the canceled check is proof that the check was written, and the amount of the check should equal the amount entered in the disbursement journal and in the monthly bank statement. Finally, the receipt, bill, or voucher establishes that the funds were expended for the authorized purpose.

Ideally, you should be able to match up with each expenditure a canceled check, a voucher (or receipt or bill), and an entry in the local union disbursement journal. The sum of the amounts of all the canceled checks for all the expenses for the audit period should equal the sum of the vouchers, bills, or receipts, which should equal the sum of the entries in the disbursement journal.

What information should I ask for?

☐ Disbursement journals or ledgers for the audit period (fig. 5–2);

☐ all canceled and voided checks for the audit period;

☐ all bank statements (checking and savings) for the audit period, including forms used to reconcile the union's book balance with the bank's balance (see fig. 5–5);

☐ all documentation (receipts, itemized bills, vouchers) for the audit period, including time and expense vouchers (fig. 5–4); and

☐ all executive board or membership meeting minutes which will establish authorization of expenses for the audit period.

General Principles for Reviewing Disbursements

Before the local union can pay out any funds, it must authorize the payment. The Landrum-Griffin Act is silent as to exactly how this authorization should occur or its form, but the fiduciary duty of all union officers, agents, and representatives is to "manage, invest and *expend* [money] in accordance with its constitution and bylaws and *any regulations of the governing bodies adopted thereunder*" (Section 501[a], Labor-Management Reporting and Disclosure Act, emphasis added).

The mechanics of how authorization occurs will vary from union to union. In some cases, the financial officer receives *blanket authorization* from the executive board to spend up to a specific amount for expenses such as rent, utilities, taxes, per capita tax payments, and clerical salaries. In other cases, authorization may have to be granted at a general membership meeting.

It is vitally important that you find out exactly what procedure for authorizing disbursements your local union uses *before* you begin your review of disbursements for the audit period. You may find the authorization procedure described in your union's constitution and bylaws. If you are not certain, ask a former trustee or your executive board.

It is not always necessary to review the authorization and documentation on every disbursement. For example, if your local union is especially large and has written a thousand checks during the time period being audited, you do not have to check the audit trail on every one. You probably don't have the time or patience to do so, much less the reason.

Some local union expenses, such as payroll taxes, occur infrequently. Other than making certain that withholding and FICA (Social Security) taxes *have* been paid, there is little need to determine whether or not there is adequate authorization or documentation. After all, the *law* requires organizations and individuals to pay taxes; it isn't voluntary.

Other local union expenses occur on a regular or *recurring* basis. Office rent, for example, is a uniform amount payable each month. This payment is usually authorized when the local union signs a lease agreement. Following the audit trail on all rent checks paid during the audit period is probably unnecessary.

Another recurring expense is per capita tax. Failure to pay per capita tax can have serious consequences; it is not as though the executive board can lightly decide not to pay it. Once again, it is probably not necessary to look for proper authorization, but you will want to be certain that the proper amount of per capita tax is being paid.

The audit trail for some other expenses probably *should* be inspected more carefully. These include travel, lost wages, telephone, furniture and equipment, supplies, and professional expenses. More specific authorization may be required, since these are typically *nonrecurring* expenses, and good documentation is required to prove that the funds were spent for their authorized purpose. Figure 5–3 lists the authorizations and documentation typically on hand or required for various expenses.

Figure 5–3
Authorization and Documentation by Disbursement

Disbursement	Authorization	Documentation
Officer/employee salaries	Executive board or membership motion to pay	Payroll voucher; time and expense voucher
Officer/employee fringe benefits	Executive board motion to approve contributions or trust fund agreement	Payroll voucher or billing statement from third-party carrier or trust fund
Lost wages for officers or stewards	Executive board motion to approve payment	Time and expense vouchers
Taxes	Motion to establish tax account or approve payment of taxes	W-2 forms for payroll deduction; copy of tax form
Travel	Motion from executive board or membership approving travel	Time and expense report with appropriate receipts
Per capita tax	Motion from executive board or membership	Copy of statement that accompanies payment of tax
Professional expenses	Motion from executive board or membership	Detailed, itemized statement of expenses
Supplies	Revolving charge; authorizing motion	Copies of invoices, billing statements, or receipts
Postage	Motion authorizing purchase of stamps, postage meter, or monthly allocation	Copies of postage meter billings or postal receipts
Telephone	Motion authorizing monthly telephone expenses up to a limit or case-by-case approval	Voucher with attached copy of the billing, with appropriate explanation
Rent	Motion authorizing lease or payment of monthly rent or mortgage	Receipt from landlord, statement of account, or mortgage
Furniture/equipment	Motion authorizing purchase of furniture or equipment	Invoice, sales receipt, or statement of account
Transfers	Motion authorizing transfer of funds	Bank statement and deposit slips showing transfer *from* and *to*

While making a distinction between recurring and nonrecurring expenses reduces the number of audit trails to follow, there still may be a lot of expenses to review and not enough time! Suppose you're satisfied with authorization and documentation on all recurring expenses, including payroll taxes, per capita taxes, and rent, but you still have eight hundred checks for nonrecurring expenses, six hundred of which are for lost wages and travel. If the prospect of following the audit trail and carefully inspecting documentation for each one is too much to bear, there is a shortcut. An acceptable auditing procedure is to take a *random sample* of all the expenses and then follow the audit trail through on each one. Here's how it works:

- ☐ Choose an expense category from which you wish to sample (example: travel, lost wages, or supplies).
- ☐ Decide the percentage of the total number of expenses in this category that you want to sample. You may want to sample one out of every three expenses (33 percent), one out of ten (10 percent), or one out of five (20 percent). The higher the percentage, the more audit trails you will have to follow, but the greater the chance that you won't miss anything unusual.
- ☐ Turning to your disbursement journal or ledger, find the beginning date of the audit period then move over to the column that corresponds to the expense category from which you want to sample.
- ☐ If you plan to take a 33 percent random sample, write down the check number for every *third* entry in this column, between the starting and ending date of the audit period. If you want to take a 10 percent random sample, write down the check number for every *tenth* entry in this column, between the starting and ending date of the audit period.
- ☐ After you have written down the check numbers, pull the canceled checks and documentation, such as receipts and vouchers, that correspond to those checks.

Whether you examine *all* expenses in *all* categories, or only a *sample* of expenses, there are basic checks you should make to ensure that there is adequate authorization, the documentation and recordkeeping is adequate, and the funds have been spent for their authorized purpose.

What Do I Do with the Audit Trail Information?

1. For each canceled check, be sure the name on the endorsement matches that of the payee (the person to whom the check was made out). You should also verify that the payee's signature matches the one on the endorsement. This routine procedure is an effective way to verify that all checks were received by the individuals or businesses they were made out to. If any checks were not endorsed by the payees, you may wish to recommend a follow-up by the local union's financial officer. Banks are not always careful about checking the identification of individuals cashing checks. Your concern here is to make sure that legitimate payments are made promptly to the party to whom money is owed.

You should also make certain that the checks have been signed by the required officers. Most local unions require at least two signatures for each check. There should be signature cards for these officers. You need to alert the union to any deviation from its policy.

2. Look for voided checks. Every check that is voided, for whatever reason, should be retained and word *VOID* clearly marked on the check. If several consecutive checks have been voided, or you cannot locate any voided checks, you should investigate further. You should also be alert for what seems to be an unreasonable number of voided checks.

If a check is marked "void" in the check register but cannot be found, it is possible that it has been stolen, lost, or written and cashed under false pretenses. You should record the check number for each voided check and see if any turn up as canceled checks. If any do, you may have to recommend that the executive board pursue legal action.

3. For each expense, verify that there is a canceled check, receipt, voucher, statement, or itemized bill, as well as an entry in the disbursement journal. The amount of the canceled check and in the journal entry should be equal to the amount on the receipt, voucher, or itemized bill.

If there is no accompanying receipt, bill, voucher, or other supporting documentation, you should bring this to the attention of the financial officer. You should also let the financial officer know if the amount of the check, in the journal entry, and on the documentation don't jibe.

4. Finally, if you have the minutes or authorizing document, check that the documentation establishes that the union funds were spent for their authorized purpose. If not, you may need to seek clarification from the financial officer.

Salaries

In local unions that hire clerical or support staff or that employ full-time officers or business agents, employees and officers are usually paid a salary. This salary may be paid on a monthly, bi-weekly, weekly, or other periodic basis. The salaries may be determined by a collective bargaining agreement or by executive board or membership resolution. If your local union uses a different form of authorization or documentation for these disbursements, you should follow it instead of the procedure described below.

The executive board or the membership, depending on how expenses are authorized, should have a motion made, properly seconded, and then voted on regarding the payment of salaries to all officers and/or employees. This motion should be recorded in the minutes of the executive board or the membership meeting. If the salary or wage is set by a collective bargaining agreement, the motion should in effect ratify the agreement and adopt the salary or wage schedule of the agreement as local union policy. In addition, the motion may require officers or employees to submit time sheets or payroll vouchers by a certain date in order to be paid. Depending on the policy, this voucher can be signed by the local union's chief executive officer, chief financial officer, or the employee's supervisor. This voucher also serves as documentation of the disbursement. Time and expense vouchers used by officers may also include travel and other expenses.

Fringe Benefits

By international or national union constitution or convention action, collective bargaining agreement, or local union action, the local union may provide certain fringe benefits to its full-time officers and employees, including but not limited to pensions, health and dental insurance, life insurance, and vacation. In addition to these benefits, some benefits, such as unemployment compensation, workers' compensation, and social security, are *legally required* and *must* be paid.

Typically, authorization for fringe benefit payments is a one-time action and is handled rather informally. If it occurs at all, it is in the form of a motion at a meeting of the executive board or local union body in such form as "moved, seconded, and approved that the local union make the required payments to all fringe benefit programs for the next calendar year for the following full-time officers and staff."

Documentation can be as basic as statements of account from the various insurance programs, such as workers' compensation premiums paid with a workers' compensation carrier, health insurance payments made to a group carrier, or vacation payments made to a jointly administered vacation trust. You should look for documentation that clearly establishes what the payment is for, on whose behalf it is made, and for what time period it is made. You should check not only that the required payments are being made in a timely manner but that all staff and full-time officers have the required coverage.

Lost Wages

The best format for documenting lost wage payments to officers and stewards is probably to require the use of a lost time voucher, shown in figure 5–4. Your union probably uses a similar form; if so, use it instead. Whatever your procedure, there should be some documentation that *at a minimum* provides the following information:

- ☐ date the lost time occurred;
- ☐ number of hours claimed (if possible, the specific hours, from what time to what time);
- ☐ wage rate per hour claimed;
- ☐ total payment claimed;
- ☐ reason for incurring the expense; and
- ☐ signature of the claimant.

This form serves as a voucher. The authorization for payment is usually made *after* the voucher has been submitted. There may be occasions when you have reason to believe that members are submitting lost wage claims for time spent "on the clock" at work. When you have such information, you may feel an investigation is worthwhile. This can be accomplished by requesting the member's time cards or payroll records for the days in question. If these records show the member was working at the same time as he or she was claiming lost wages, you have the evidence you need. This should be reported to the financial officer or executive board for further action.

Taxes

State and federal withholding taxes must also be paid on a regular basis, either quarterly or, in larger unions, more frequently. Normally, a set of *tax tables* is used to compute the amount of withholding to be taken from each

Figure 5–4
Sample Lost Wages and Expense Voucher

Name: *Joe March* Social Security #: *222-11-3344*
Purpose of union business: *Prepare/attend arbitration hearing*
Beginning date: *November 1, 1991*
Ending date: *December 1, 1991*

Date	Lost time from work (Hrs.)	Pay rate	Subtotal
11/3/91	8.0	$11.25	$90.00
11/4/91	8.0	$11.25	$90.00
11/8/91	4.0	$11.25	$45.00
11/9/91	8.0	$11.25	$90.00
Totals	28.0		$315.00
FICA			$23.66
Federal W/H			$87.25
State W/H			$49.25
Other			$0.00
Net Pay			$154.84

Expenses

Type	Date	Amount
Hotel		$0.00
Meals	See attached receipts	$12.50
Mileage	See attached	$13.86
Telephone	Phone bill attached	$3.62
Other		$0.00
Total expenses		$29.98
Net pay and expenses		$184.82
Voucher #		1378
Check #		1378

President's signature ______________________________

Financial secretary's signature ______________________________ officer's or employee's check, as well as from lost wage checks. Individuals must notify the local union's financial officer regarding the number of deductions they wish to use. Knowing the number of deductions and the pay period used (monthly, bi-weekly, weekly, or other), it is possible to look up the required amount of withholding for each check. These amounts are added up and a check is sent to the state or federal tax office. In some cases, special tax accounts can be set up with your bank.

Withholding the proper amounts is critically important. Federal and state tax authorities have the right to audit local union books to make certain that the proper amount of taxes is being withheld. Unemployment insurance and workers' compensation carriers also have this right. You may wish to select one or two pay periods in which to verify that the proper amount of state and federal taxes is being withheld from paychecks.

Travel

Travel authorizations are typically handled on a case-by-case basis, except in large local unions whose officers and employees travel frequently to conduct union business. Normally, a motion is made, seconded, and approved authorizing an officer, employee, or delegate to attend a meeting, conference, class, or convention, and sums of money are specified in that motion. A typical motion might read: "Two delegates are authorized to attend the meeting, with two days lost wages, two nights lodging in one double room, mileage to and from the meeting at the rate of $0.20 per mile, with reimbursement of meals for those two days provided that receipts are furnished and the reimbursement shall not exceed twenty dollars per day." This typical motion would constitute authorization for the travel expenses.

In some cases, travel is authorized on a blanket basis. There are several ways in which this can be done. Officers or staff who must service contracts or visit shops where members work may be authorized a regular travel allowance or perhaps a vehicle allowance. Depending on how this blanket authorization is worded, officers may have to submit supporting documentation or mileage logs. In some cases, a daily expense allowance to cover such routine expenses as parking, tolls, meals, and related transportation expenses may be authorized.

Regardless of how such blanket authorizations are worded, the officer or staff member normally is required to submit a voucher or claim for expenses. This voucher then constitutes the required documentation.

When receipts are required for lodging, transportation, and meals, they should be original receipts, with the date, place, and amount clearly legible. If more than one person is covered by the receipt, the names of the individuals covered should be written on the receipt. A restaurant or motel receipt is preferable to a credit card receipt, which does not itemize expenses. Itemization is especially important when authorization does not cover spouses, alcoholic beverages, or other amenities. The local union needs to be certain that expenses beyond those that have been authorized are not being reimbursed.

Receipts for all travel, lodging, and meals should be attached to the expense voucher (see fig. 5–4). The local union may wish to prepay hotel and transportation expenses by check when possible. This ensures that adequate documentation is available for these expenses, and if staff, officers, or members wish to expend their own funds for items not covered by the authorization, they are free to do so without later having to separate covered and noncovered expenses from the receipts.

Per Capita Taxes

Per capita taxes may be the largest single disbursement the local union makes. Per capita taxes here include payments made to national or international unions, regional or district bodies, and central and state labor councils. Authorizations are not as important as for travel, lost wages, supplies, and professional expenses because the local union has little choice about whether to pay these taxes. Therefore, you should not spend too much time looking up authorizations for per capita tax payments. Payments to local or state central bodies, depending on constitutional requirements, may allow more discretion on the part of the local union.

Documentation for per capita taxes normally consists of a copy of the payment voucher or per capita reporting form that accompanies the check for monthly or regular per capita payments. You can simply compare the number of members reported for the month with the records you used to establish the amount of dues owed in a particular month.

Professional Expenses

Professional expenses include payments made to attorneys, accountants, and consultants for professional services performed. Authorization for these expenses is normally quite specific and is easily located in the minutes of the executive board or membership body. In the case of legal representation, a resolution may have been passed several years ago authorizing payment of a retainer to the law firm. If the amount of the retainer should change, normally a new resolution would be required. If the law firm will need to bill the local union for work over and above the amount of the retainer, this may also require a separate authorization. Consultant and accountant fees are normally one-time authorizations, although a local union may keep an accounting firm on retainer for assistance in bookkeeping matters.

Documentation should clearly establish the purpose of the disbursement, as well as the date the services were performed and the total amount charged. The more detailed this statement, the better. As a trustee, you need to establish clearly that the service was for the benefit of the local union and its members. You should not be hesitant to ask for additional information, particularly since the local union is paying for the service.

Supplies

Authorization practices on supplies vary considerably. In larger local unions, there may be a revolving charge with an office supply vendor from which supplies are ordered and delivered as needed. Office supplies include expendable items, such as paper, envelopes, pencils, pens, staples, and paper clips. In this case, you may have to dig through several years of minutes to find the original authorization.

At the other extreme, smaller local unions may have to authorize each purchase of office supplies. In some cases, such as union letterhead and envelopes, the supplier may be the national or international union. Normally, this authorization is still found in the minutes.

In all cases, the documentation will consist of an invoice or billing statement that should clearly itemize the supplies purchased. Make certain that the amount on this invoice or bill equals the amount shown in the disbursement journal and on the canceled check.

Postage

Large local unions may own or lease a postage meter, while smaller unions may simply purchase a roll of stamps. Whatever the practice, the authorization should be the same. Normally, it should be found in the local union minutes, unless the chief financial officer of the local union has a blanket authorization for normal office expenses.

For purchases of stamps, express mail, faxes, and special delivery, you should obtain a receipt from the post office, delivery service, or faxing service. It would be helpful to write down the check number and the date of the check used to pay for this postage or to reimburse an officer or employee of the local union who made the purchase.

Telephone

Copies of the telephone bill should be attached to each payment voucher or maintained on file. Once again, it is a good idea to write the check number and date of the check used to pay the bill on the billing statement. Authorization to pay telephone bills usually comes in the form of an executive board or membership body motion, although sometimes the authority to disburse funds for routine office expenses is delegated by the governing body to the chief financial officer.

If an officer makes telephone calls from his or her personal phone and these calls are for authorized union business, the officer or employee should attach a copy of the telephone bill with these calls underlined or circled. A copy of this bill should be attached to the reimbursement voucher and maintained as documentation.

Rent

If the local union rents office or meeting space, there should be a lease agreement on file together with an authorizing resolution. When the rent increases, a new authorization may be required. These authorizations can be found in the local's minutes.

You should make certain that a receipt is issued for payment of each month's rent and that the check number and date of the check used to pay the rent is recorded on the receipt.

Furniture and Office Equipment

Authorizations are generally required for purchases of nonexpendable furniture and office equipment, such as desks, telephones, answering machines, copy machines, tables, chairs, and related items. These authorizations can also be found in the minutes. Documentation will consist of the invoice or billing statement, which should be retained in the files. It is wise to write the check number and date of the check used to pay for these items on the billing statement. Make certain the amount on the invoice or billing statement equals the amount of the canceled check and entry in the disbursement journal.

Transfers

As discussed earlier, transfers are often made from savings into checking accounts and vice versa. Transfers do not leave the same audit trail as checks. Like checks, there must be authorization, but there is no payee (since you're transferring money), no canceled check. Transfers from savings into checking accounts are normally made to cover cash shortages or purchases of major items. Transfers from checking to savings normally reflect special projects, or savings plans. Both transfers require governing body action, so you should be able to find authorization for these transfers in the minutes. Documentation of these transfers is provided by the bank statements for both the checking and the savings accounts. Make certain the transfer from one account is documented, as well as the transfer into the other account. If both are not documented, the bank should be contacted.

In summary, make certain the documentation clearly establishes the amount paid and that it agrees with the amount recorded in the disbursement journal and on the canceled check. You should alert the financial officer if there are *any* discrepancies here. Finally, the documentation should contain sufficient detail to identify beyond question the nature of the goods or services that were purchased.

The Last Step

Having verified the authorizations and documentation for expenses (all or a sample) for the audit period, you are probably ready to stop, but you should do one last thing. You need to be sure that the bank's balance of the union's checking account equals the union's balance. To do this, you need to obtain and closely examine the monthly bank statement that covers the audit period. Figure 5–5 contains a sample reconciliation form. If the bank's balance and the union's book balance are not equal, there may have been math errors, checks may not have cleared, or checks may not have been properly voided. Any discrepancies should be carefully examined by the financial officer. Once you have verified that your book's balance equals the bank's, you can begin your next audit period with the books balanced.

Figure 5–5
Sample Reconciliation Form

1.	Starting date	January 2, 1991
2.	Ending date	February 1, 1991
3.	Account number	A643795-003
4.	Bank balance at end of period	$2,345.12
5.	Income received and added to book balance but not yet deposited	+ $ 45.00
6.	Deposits made before end of period that do not appear on statement	+ $ 0.00
7.	Subtract checks written and subtracted from book balance before the end of the period which don't appear on the bank statement	– $ 124.79
8.	Adjusted bank account balance	$ 2,265.33
9.	Bank account balance shown in *union books*	$ 2,273.33
10.	Bank service charges listed on statement but not yet subtracted from union's book balance	– $ 8.00
11.	Subtract debit memos listed on bank statement but not yet subtracted from book balance	– $ 0.00
12.	Amounts appearing on bank statement but not yet entered in union books	(+/-) $ 0.00
13.	Adjusted book balance for this account	$ 2,265.33
14.	Subtract line 13 from line 8	$ 0.00
15.	If line 14 equals zero, you have reconciled your book and bank balances for this account.	

Exercises for Chapter 5

Using the tools provided in this chapter, answer the following questions, and explain your answers.

1. After reviewing the monthly checking account reconciliation forms, you discover that three checks to an office supply company have been outstanding for more than five months. What should you do?

2. After reviewing all checks for the audit period, you find that checks with the following numbers were voided: 313, 314, 316. You also cannot find the last two checks (314 and 316). What should you do?

3. In October 1990, the executive board authorized a transfer of $500 from the local union's savings account into checking for the purpose of covering additional office expenses. In your audit, you find a deposit slip showing that the money was deposited into checking, but in your review of the bank records you find that no money was transferred out of the savings account. What should you do, and why?

4. Check number 1310 was written to the law firm of Wilson and Smith. The documentation is a letter dated August 14 that requests payment for "legal research and consultation, over and above the monthly retainer, in the amount of $850." Your review of executive board minutes and other records shows only that a monthly retainer of $750 was authorized. You also find a canceled check and entry for the month for Wilson and Smith for $1600.

Is this adequate documentation, and do you think there was sufficient authorization for this disbursement?

5. As a trustee, you have received complaints that two stewards have been filing lost wage requests while they were "on the clock" at work during the month of December. You obtain payroll records for this period, as well as all lost wage vouchers for December, and discover the following:

Lost Wage Claim					Payroll Records	
Steward	**Date**	**Start**	**Stop**	**Lost Hours**	**Start**	**Stop**
Dickson	12/12	9:00 A.M.	3:00 P.M.	5.5	7:00 A.M.	3:30 P.M.
Dickson	12/19	11:00 A.M.	2:00 P.M.	2.5	7:00 A.M.	3:30 P.M.
Martin	12/17	9:00 A.M.	1:00 P.M.	3.5	7:00 A.M.	3:30 P.M.
Martin	12/31	1:30 P.M.	2:30 P.M.	1.0	7:00 A.M.	3:30 P.M.

What should you do about this discrepancy?

6. On November 11, 1990, the executive board authorized purchase of a new personal computer system with a wide-carriage printer and monochrome monitor and necessary accounting and word processing software for $5,265.35 after a bidding process was completed and the lowest qualified bidder selected. In reviewing union records, you learn the following:

a. A purchase order reveals the delivery was made on December 1 and included a VGA color monitor (not a monochrome monitor as spelled out in the resolution) as well as the ordered software and hardware.

b. A canceled check and journal entry to the vendor is made out in the amount of $5,435.00.

What action, if any, should you take, and why?

7. Minutes for the March 23, 1990, membership meeting reveal that the local authorized two delegates to attend a two-day regional union meeting. The resolution authorized the local union to pay lost wages for three days, mileage at $0.20 per mile, the conference fee, the bill for a double occupancy room, and receipted meals not to exceed $30 per day for each of the three days.

In reviewing the vouchers submitted by both delegates as part of your audit, you see that copies of the motel bill are attached to one voucher and mileage information is included in the other. In addition, both delegates claim the full $30 per day meals but have not attached receipts. Both vouchers look correct, as do the lost wage expenses for the three-day period for both delegates.

What action, if any, should you take at this point, and why?

6
Completing Your Audit

In this chapter, we'll examine what you do after you have completed your review of union records:

- ☐ How should you summarize your results?
- ☐ How should you present your report?
- ☐ How should you handle discrepancies and problems?

One word of caution is needed before we proceed. Your constitution and bylaws may specify a procedure for how audits or trustee reports are to be handled. If a specific format is not spelled out in your constitution and bylaws, your local union may have passed a resolution or have an established practice for how these matters should be handled. It is important that you find out if any such custom, practice, or procedure exists before you prepare and present your report. Some local unions have their own ways of handling these matters. If you aren't sure whom to ask, start with former union trustees or auditors or your executive board. You should also obtain a copy of the previous audit report. Look this over carefully to see how the information was presented, what it included, and what you think it *should* now include.

If there is a procedure laid down for reporting the information from your audit, you should follow it. Some international and national unions, such as the Allied Industrial Workers (see chap. 2) or the International Woodworkers of America, provide their local unions with specific *forms* for this purpose. If there isn't a specific procedure or set of forms to be used, the information in this chapter may be helpful.

Summarizing Your Results

The local union executive board will want some written documentation that the auditors or trustees have indeed examined the financial records. This report should indicate, at a minimum, what records were examined and what was found. There is no common format or procedure here; the práctice will vary from union to union.

In some unions, trustees simply sign their names in the cash and disbursement journals after completing the audit; in others, the results are reported at either a local executive board or a general membership meeting and are recorded in the minutes. In still other unions, such as the Elevator Constructors (see chap. 2), a written report is mailed to the membership. It is vitally important that you find out beforehand how your results should be summarized and presented.

Assuming that there is no established format in your local union for summarizing the findings of your audit, the following is a recommended format for doing so.

In summarizing the results of your audit or review of your union's financial records, you should, *at the minimum*, cover the following:

☐ Who were the auditors or trustees who participated in the audit?

☐ What *time period* did the audit report cover (one year, six months, one month)? What were the beginning and ending dates of the audit period?

☐ *What records* did you examine? Normally, the scope of the audit is determined by your constitution, bylaws, resolutions, tradition, and past practice. If there is no clear definition of what records need to be reviewed, however, you should list these records very carefully in summarizing the report. This is very important if you do not examine all financial records. If you audited only a *random sample* of expenses or dues income, you should *clearly* state this.

☐ Was all *income* properly *accounted for*? Did the amount of income (dues, fees, rent, sales, interest, etc.) owed equal the amount of income *actually* collected? Were receipts properly issued for all payments to the local union? Were there any discrepancies?

- ☐ Were all local union *assets* properly *accounted for*? Were there adequate records to establish the value of all the assets the local union holds?

- ☐ Were all *disbursements* properly authorized, and was there adequate documentation to establish that all moneys were paid out in accordance with those authorizations?

- ☐ What *discrepancies or problems* were there, if any? What recommendations, if any, do you have for the union and the union's financial officer to improve recordkeeping and accountability?

Figure 6–1 is a sample form for providing this information. You can attach *copies* of your worksheets (for example, figs. 3–4 through 3–11) to this report. If you use computerized spreadsheets for your audit, you can print out copies of these spreadsheets and attach them to the report. If you use a calculator, it may be worthwhile to attach the paper tapes showing your totals.

Recommendations for addressing problems might include the following:

- ☐ That financial officers and employees be instructed to issue receipts for *all* payments received by the local union;

- ☐ that equipment and furniture inventories be conducted more frequently;

- ☐ that new or modified expense vouchers be developed;

- ☐ that there be increased monitoring of payment authorizations; and

- ☐ that financial officers and employees be given additional training.

Any recommendations you make in your report should be supported by evidence you uncovered in your audit investigation.

Figure 6–1
Format for an Audit Summary Report

1. Names of union auditors who participated in the audit:

____________________________ ____________________________

____________________________ ____________________________

2. Beginning date of audit period:__________________________________

3. Ending date of audit period:____________________________________

4. What records were examined (check those below)?

a. Cash journals_____

b. Receipt books_____

c. Deposit slips_____

d. Property deeds_____

e. Checking account records_____

f. Savings accounts_____

g. Expense vouchers_____

h. Reimbursement receipts_____

i. Inventories_____

j. Disbursement journals_____

5. *Income* (attach worksheets, figs. 3–5 to 3–11)

a. Did the income *owed* for each income source below equal the income *actually collected* (check "Yes" or "No")?

Dues	Yes___	No___
Fees and assessments	Yes___	No___
Fines	Yes___	No___
Interest and dividends	Yes___	No___
Sales of union supplies	Yes___	No___
Rental income	Yes___	No___
Loan repayments	Yes___	No___
Vending machine sales	Yes___	No___
Sale of union assets	Yes___	No___
Other (list:)	Yes___	No___

b. Were receipts properly issued for all income sources?

c. What discrepancies/problems were found in income accounting?

6. *Assets* (attach worksheets)

a. Were there adequate records to establish the value of all assets held by the union (check one)?

Yes___ No___ If "no," what problems were found?

b. Was there an adequate inventory of union furniture and equipment (check one)?

Yes___ No___ If "no," what problems were found?

c. What discrepancies/problems were found in asset accounting?

7. *Disbursements* (attach worksheets)

a. Were all disbursements properly authorized?

Yes___ No___ If "no," what problems existed?

b. Was there adequate documentation for all expense items?

Yes___ No___ If "no," what problems existed?

c. Were there any other discrepancies/problems in the area of disbursements?

8. What recommendations do you have for addressing the problems you encountered?

9. Do you have any other recommendations about how to improve financial recordkeeping and accounting?

[Signatures of trustees and dates here]

Presenting Your Report

Once again, you should check with your executive board to find out how your report should be presented. Normally, the report goes directly to the executive board, but this will vary from union to union. In many cases, submitting the audit report is a mere formality, unless problems or discrepancies are discovered that require executive board or membership action.

Assuming there is no established or recommended procedure for presenting your report, here are some suggestions:

1. *If the report is presented to the executive board:*

   ☐ Provide copies of the report to board members *in advance* of the meeting, so they have time to study it. If advance distribution is not possible, ensure that board members have a copy in front of them during your presentation. This makes it easier for them to follow along and ask questions if necessary.

   ☐ Have all trustees or auditors present at the meeting and available for questions.

   ☐ If you don't know the answer to a question, don't make up an answer; say "I'm not sure." You should then confer with other trustees and check out the facts; then you can respond. You may have to get back to the questioner later.

   ☐ Try to keep the presentation short, allowing plenty of time for discussion, particularly if you have recommendations.

2. *If your presentation involves the general membership*:

   ☐ You may wish to use a blackboard, flip chart, overhead transparencies, or slides to present detailed information.

   ☐ You may wish to distribute copies of the report to the membership at the meeting, if you feel it is appropriate. You should first consult with your executive board and financial officer regarding distribution of materials.

   ☐ Have all trustees attend the meeting and be available for questions.

   ☐ If you don't know the answer to a question, don't

make up an answer; it is much more honest and effective to say "I'm not sure." You can then confer with your fellow trustees, review the records, and get back to the questioner later.

☐ Try to keep the presentation short, but allow plenty of time for discussion, particularly if you have recommendations.

☐ Once the audit report has been presented and the questions answered, a motion is usually made to accept the report. This motion is then voted on by the executive board if a proper second is made.

3. *If you make a written report to the executive board:*

Use a standard format, similar to the one shown in figure 6–1. You should include a cover letter (see fig. 6–2) for transmittal of the report. The letter should be on union letterhead, dated and signed by all trustees. It should be addressed to the chief executive officer of the union (in some unions, this is the president; in others, it is the financial secretary-treasurer).

Figure 6–2
Sample Cover Letter for Transmitting Audit Report to Local Union

Date

Dear (local union officers):

Attached please find a copy of the audit report prepared by the undersigned trustees for the period beginning ____________ and ending____________. We would like to thank the financial officer and ________________________ for their valuable assistance in obtaining and reviewing all the necessary records and answering questions.

We hope this report will be useful, and we will be happy to answer any questions regarding it that you may have.

In solidarity,

[Signatures of the trustees]

Handling Discrepancies and Problems

If your review of your union's financial records uncovers any discrepancies (over- or undercollection of income, missing records or receipts, inappropriate authorization, inadequate documentation, or other problems), it is the duty of the trustees to point out these problems to the governing body of the local union. This is part of the trustees' and officers' *fiduciary* duty to the union and its members. Remember, if such problems are noted but not corrected, the union and its officers may be sued in federal court by any member. This duty to inform your executive board of problems should therefore not be taken lightly.

There is no one best way to handle discrepancies or problems. You should first of all check your union constitution and bylaws, as well as any resolutions that might address this area. In addition, former trustees or ones with more experience may have established customs or practices for handling problems.

While it is important to bring problems and discrepancies to the attention of the appropriate union officers and board members, it is equally, if not more important, to have *all* your facts straight *before* doing so. What appears to be a major problem may indeed have a perfectly reasonable explanation. The key is not to act until you have *all the facts*. Unions urge employers not to act until they have all the facts; this doesn't give trustees a license to do what employers are often criticized of doing.

Once you have gathered all the necessary information and documentation, *ask questions* and *seek clarification*. If something doesn't look right, don't jump the gun! First identify who in the union might be able to provide the necessary information or documentation, and then *ask* that individual. This should always be your next step.

If this step clears up the problem or provides the information you need, you have accomplished your task. If it doesn't, you can simply tell the individual involved that if a satisfactory answer or information is not provided, you are prepared to put this in your report and to inform the governing board of the union. You should also state that you hope that this won't be necessary. The threat of taking a problem to a higher level is often all that is needed to clear it up. Such conversations should be conducted in the presence of a witness or the information communicated in writing, to establish that you made an attempt to resolve the issue informally.

If this option is not successful in clearing up the problem, the final step is to put the matter in your written report. And when you do so, you can confidently state that you tried your level best to clear the matter up with the person involved but were not successful. You cannot be criticized for making an "end run" around this individual, and you have shown good faith in trying to resolve the matter.

It is important to realize that as a trustee, you are not an *outside investigator*. You are part of the union. At the same time, once you have made your audit report, your job is done. It is not up to you and your fellow trustees or auditors to put the recommendations you make into practice. That is the responsibility of the union's governing body or executive board.

It is not appropriate for trustees or auditors to first make a statement to the press, the U.S. Department of Labor, or the National Labor Relations Board regarding discrepancies or problems uncovered by your audit. *Your job* is to *report*; the *executive board's* responsibility is to *act*. This doesn't mean you can't try to influence them in this matter, just as any other member of the union is free to do so. The bottom line is that you are an investigator, *not a judge or jury*.

Answers to Exercises

Chapter 2

1. **False**

The rights and responsibilities of union trustees can be found ONLY in the Landrum-Griffin Act. Union constitutions and bylaws also specify rights and responsibilities of union trustees and auditors.

2. **False**

According to the LMRDA, trustees always have the authority to co-sign checks and loans for their local union. The LMRDA gives no such authority to trustees; it doesn't even mention them by name. This authority would come only from a union's constitution or bylaws.

3. **False**

Regardless of their union's constitution and bylaws, members can direct their trustees to audit union books at any time. Only the union constitution and bylaws or very special circumstances can bring about special audits.

4. **False**

Trustees have a responsibility to see that union moneys are used solely for the benefit of the members. Trustees *also* have a fiduciary responsibility to ensure that union funds are used for the sole benefit of the *union and* its members.

5. **A**

If any discrepancies are found in local union financial records during the audit, they should first be reported to: (circle one)

The local union financial officer should always be the first person alerted to any potential or actual discrepancies.

6. **E**

If your financial officer refuses to show you a part of the books or records you need for your audit, what should you do? (circle one)

This may depend upon the union's constitution and bylaws, but the local union executive board is the most logical choice here.

Chapter 3

1a. What do you think is wrong? It would seem that you have not collected enough money (the amount owed for the period is greater than the amount collected).

1b. What might have caused this to happen? There are several possible explanations: one or more members didn't pay enough dues; your records about the amount owed are incorrect; or money was collected but there was no receipt or entry made in the cash journal.

1c. What do you think needs to be done? First, double-check your records to be sure that the amount owed reflects all the members who really do owe dues for the audit period. Next, make certain that the receipts issued to self-payers jibe with the journal entries. If you have done this and you are still $55 dollars off, it would appear that not only has somebody not paid dues but that somebody else has paid the wrong amount. You can reach this conclusion because $55 divided by $18.50 does not give an even number ($18.50 x 3 = $55.50), suggesting that perhaps somebody paid $0.50 short of full dues.

You will have to match the list of people who owe against people who paid. If the amount owed by one person equals the amount collected, you can scratch this person off the list. When you find that the amount owed for an individual *doesn't* equal the amount paid, you have found your *suspect*!

2a. What do you think is wrong? According to the worksheet, you should have collected dues for 524 members (the number who *owe*), but you actually collected on 514. Thus, you are 10 members or $232.50 short.

2b. What might have caused this to happen? Since this is a monthly payroll deduction, the employer may have made an error. This may have occurred because the employer made a mistake on several deductions or didn't have the right information to deduct dues properly, or there may have been an error in *your* records; perhaps a member started working later than his dues card indicates or somebody quit a month earlier than you said.

Don't automatically assume that the employer has made a mistake when it might be your records that are wrong.

2c. What do you think needs to be done? First, make certain that your records are correct. Bring this matter to your financial officer's attention and offer your assistance if you feel so inclined. If the union's records are in error, they should be corrected. These corrected records can then be compared with the employer's records. If this resolves the difference, that should take care of this month's problem, but there may be similar problems for the rest of the audit period. You should then be prepared to repeat this procedure for additional pay periods or months of the audit period.

If upon investigation by your financial officer, your records are error free, or do not totally explain the difference, the employer's records may be in error. You might suggest to the financial officer that a meeting be scheduled with the employer to discuss these problems and to see what can be done. Depending upon contract language and local practice, you will probably want to seek recovery of the dues that should have been paid but weren't.

3a. What do you think is wrong? Based on the worksheet, it would appear that you have collected more than is actually owed. But before you jump to conclusions, check your records first!

3b. What might have caused this to happen? If your records are indeed accurate, somebody may have paid twice or otherwise overpaid. If your records are not accurate, then a recordkeeping problem may have caused the overpayment. Perhaps a receipt was not issued or an entry made in the cash journal. Finally, the overpayment may have resulted from carryover from a previous audit period that was not properly credited to that period.

3c. What do you think needs to be done? Assuming your records are accurate, you will have to find the individual who overpaid. As in problem 1, check the list of individuals who *owed* fines, fees, or assessments. Then go through the receipts book or cash journal for the period and, by each name, write down the amount *actually collected*. If the amount collected equals the amount owed, scratch the name off the list. But if the amount collected is *greater than* the amount owed, then this individual has overpaid.

4a. What do you think is wrong? The amount collected is $180 less than the amount owed.

4b. What might have caused this to happen? Either your records are in error or somebody didn't pay his or her rent. Check you records first to be sure you're not missing something.

4c. What do you think needs to be done? After you have eliminated the possibility that your records are in error (talk to the officer who books space or rents out offices; he or she should have a log, ledger, or file of renters), you should write down all the renters for the audit period and what they owed. Then, turning to the receipts book or the cash journal, find out exactly what each paid for the period. Write this amount down next to the amount each *owed* for the period. If the amount owed equals the amount collected, scratch his or her name off the list. If the amount owed is greater than the amount collected, the renter didn't pay and owes the local money. Somebody may even have paid who shouldn't have.

Chapter 4

1. Completed depreciation schedule with boldface type showing answers:

	Telephones	**Typewriter**	
Year Purchased	1989	1990	
Sales Price	$125.00	$300.00	
First-Year Value	$100.00	$240.00	
Second-Year Value	**$75.00**	**$180.00**	
Third-Year Value	**$50.00**	**$120.00**	
Fourth-Year Value	**$25.00**	**$60.00**	
Fifth-Year Value	**$0.00**	**$0.00**	

2. Your review of inventory records for the local union reveals that a telephone answering machine was purchased in 1988 and entered on the inventory in that year and in 1989. But you cannot find it on the inven-

tory for 1990, and there is no record of its sale in the cash journal and there is no receipt. What should you do?

It would appear that one of three things has happened: somebody is "borrowing" the answering machine and didn't bother to let the union know that he or she is borrowing it; the answering machine has been lost, stolen, or destroyed; or the machine has been sold or donated to another organization.

The first thing to do is raise this matter with the union financial officer. You might want to suggest that the matter be raised at the next executive board meeting to determine who might have "borrowed" the machine and ask that it be returned by the end of the week. If the machine doesn't turn up by that date, you can safely assume that the machine has not been borrowed.

Next, you should look through your cash journal and receipts book to determine whether or not the answering machine has been sold since 1989. If so, an entry should show up in the cash book, and, one hopes, a receipt would have been issued to the seller. You may also want to look through executive board minutes to determine whether or not the board authorized a sale or a donation.

Finally, if you have property or renter's insurance on your office, you may want to file a claim with the insurance company. This requires a police investigation. Moreover, the deductible on your insurance policy is probably higher than the cost of a new answering machine. You may simply have to recommend that the union purchase a new answering machine.

3. A small savings account that was opened ten years ago has been inactive for some time, and you discover a copy of the passbook and signature cards during your audit. No one on the executive board is aware of this account, and the balance is $500. What should you do?

This looks like a nice little windfall, but be careful! First, you should visit the bank and verify that the account is still active, since some banks close inactive accounts. While you're at the bank, obtain a complete account history so you can determine whether or not there has been any activity in the account over the last ten years. If there has been, this should be noted and brought to the attention of the financial secretary-treasurer. There may have been *more* money in here, but some of it may have been withdrawn.

The bottom line is that somebody was asleep at the switch. This is the reason you should verify the disposition of *all* the local union accounts and liquid assets as part of your audit. Whether it is $50, $500, or $5,000, this money probably could have been put to better use than sitting in a passbook.

Chapter 5

1. After reviewing the monthly checking account reconciliation forms (fig. 5–4), you discover that three checks to an office supply company have been outstanding for more than five months. What should you do ?

Bring this to the immediate attention of the financial officer. S/he should call the office supply company to find out what is going on. In some cases, where the amount of money involved is sufficient, you may wish to stop payment on the checks, but the bank will charge you for this service.

2. After reviewing all checks for the audit period, you find that checks with the following numbers were voided: 313, 314, 316. You also cannot find the last two checks (314 and 316). What should you do?

This should be brought to the attention of the financial officer immediately.

3. In October 1990, the executive board authorized a transfer of $500 from the local union's savings account into checking for the purpose of covering additional office expenses. In your audit, you find a deposit slip showing that the money was deposited into checking, but your review of the bank records shows no transfer occurring out of the savings account. What should you do, and why?

First, bring this to the attention of the financial officer. In all likelihood, this is a bank error that can be resolved by a telephone call to the bank. All savings account statements from October 1990 should be checked, however, to see if the transfer withdrawal shows up there.

4. Check number 1310 was written to the law firm of Wilson and Smith. The documentation is a letter dated August 14 that requests payment for "legal research and consultation, over and above the monthly retainer, in the amount of $850." Your review of executive board minutes and other records shows only that a monthly retainer of $750 was authorized. You also find a canceled check and entry for the month for Wilson and Smith for $1600.

Is this adequate documentation, and do you think there was sufficient authorization for this disbursement?

First, bring this up with your financial officer, and see what he or she knows about this matter. On the surface, the letter from the law firm doesn't provide enough detail, and the authorization only mentions a monthly retainer and says nothing about additional legal research or consultation. You need more information about the authorization. Besides checking this out, you may need more detail from the law firm regarding exactly what research and consultation were provided, for whom, and on what dates.

5. As a trustee, you have received complaints that two stewards have been filing lost wage requests while they were "on the clock" at work during the month of December. You obtain payroll records for this period, as well as all lost wage vouchers for December, and discover the following.

Lost Wage Claim					Payroll Records	
Steward	**Date**	**Start**	**Stop**	**Lost Hours**	**Start**	**Stop**
Dickson	12/12	9:00 A.M.	3:00 P.M.	5.5	7:00 A.M.	3:30 P.M.
Dickson	12/19	11:00 A.M.	2:00 P.M.	2.5	7:00 A.M.	3:30 P.M.
Martin	12/17	9:00 A.M.	1:00 P.M.	3.5	7:00 A.M.	3:30 P.M.
Martin	12/31	1:30 P.M.	2:30 P.M.	1.0	7:00 A.M.	3:30 P.M.

What should you do about this discrepancy?

It would appear that Dickson and Martin have claimed lost wages from the union for hours that they also were "on the clock"; it seems they were "double-dipping." Martin claimed 4.5 hours of lost wages for time that he was working for the company, and Dickson claimed 8 hours of lost wages while on the clock. Your first move after documenting this apparent discrepancy should be to call this to the attention of your local's financial officer or executive board. You are not the jury or judge here, not even the prosecuting attorney. It is up to the executive board to decide what to do, but they do have, as do you, a fiduciary responsibility to make sure that funds are not misused.

6. On November 11, 1990, the executive board authorized purchase of a new personal computer system with a wide-carriage printer and monochrome monitor and necessary accounting and word processing software for $5,265.35 after a bidding process was completed and the lowest qualified bidder selected. In reviewing union records, you learn the following:

a. A purchase order reveals the delivery was made on December 1 and included a VGA color monitor (not a monochrome monitor as spelled out in the resolution) as well as the ordered software and hardware.

b. A canceled check and journal entry to the vendor is made in the amount of $5,435.

What action, if any, should you take, and why?

When you compare the purchase order with the authorization, you see that equipment *other than* that which was authorized was delivered. In fact, the executive board specifically authorized purchase of a monochrome, not a color VGA, monitor. But more important, the authorization specified an exact price, and the price of the delivered goods was higher than this authorized price.

You should bring this discrepancy to the attention of the financial officer or the executive board. The executive board may decide to modify its authorization and approve the purchase as is or to return the color VGA monitor for a monochrome. But this will be up to the executive board to decide.

It is normally within their rights to modify authorizations or any resolution, for that matter. The Landrum-Griffin Act requires that funds be spent in accordance with the constitution, bylaws, and *resolutions* of the governing body of the union.

7. Minutes for the March 23, 1990, membership meeting reveal that the local authorized two delegates to attend a two-day regional union meeting. The resolution authorized the local union to pay lost wages for three days, mileage at $0.20 per mile, the conference fee, the bill for a double occupancy room, and receipted meals not to exceed $30 per day for each of the three days.

In reviewing the vouchers submitted by both delegates as part of your audit, you see that copies of the motel bill are attached to one voucher and mileage information is included in the other. In addition, both delegates claim the full $30 per day meals but have not attached receipts. Both vouchers look correct, as do the lost wage expenses for the three-day period for both delegates.

What action, if any, should you take at this point, and why?

This situation illustrates why it is so important to compare documentation with the original authorization to make sure that union funds were spent only for their authorized purpose. All you can do is point out the discrepancy regarding the lack of meal receipts and recommend that the delegates be asked to furnish the necessary receipts or documentation.